Veggies Tonight –
Without a Fight!

Do your children refuse to eat anything that resembles a healthy food? Are you tired of begging and bribing? Want peace at the dinner table? It's time to become a Sneaky Chef—*the trick is to hide the foods kids* should *eat in the dishes they* will *eat.* With over 75 simple recipes, *The Sneaky Chef* is chock full of strategies for ingeniously disguising "Superfoods" in kids' favorite meals. Author Missy Chase Lapine reveals how a few simple make-ahead purees or clever replacements (some may surprise you!) can change the way your family eats. With every sneaky bite, parents will pack more fiber, whole grains, vitamins, and antioxidants in their kids' daily diets.

the SNEAKY chef™

BY MISSY CHASE LAPINE

The Sneaky Chef

Simple Strategies for Hiding Healthy Foods

in Kids' Favorite Meals

BY MISSY CHASE LAPINE

RUNNING PRESS
PHILADELPHIA • LONDON

9 8 7 6 5 4 3 2 1

Digit on the right indicates the number of this printing

Library of Congress Control Number: 20066940107

ISBN-13: 978-0-7624-3437-4

Scholastic Edition

Cover design by Bill Jones

Interior design by Alicia Freile

Edited by Jennifer Kasius

Author photo by Scott Calman

Food photos by Jerry Errico

Food Styling by Brian Preston-Campbell

Logo by Kristopher Weber

Typography: Garth Graphic and Sassoon

The ideas, methods, and suggestions contained in this book are not intended to replace the advice of a nutritionist, doctor, or other trained health professional. You should consult your Pediatrician before adopting the methods of this book. Any additions to, or changes in diet, are at the reader's discretion.

This book may be ordered by mail from the publisher.

Please include $2.50 for postage and handling.

But try your bookstore first!

Running Press Book Publishers

2300 Chestnut Street

Philadelphia, PA 19103-4371

Visit us on the web!

www.runningpress.com

This book is dedicated to your family and to my loves, Rick, Emily and Samantha, who inspire me every day.

Table of Contents

Chapter 6: Make-Ahead Recipes 93

The Recipes

Breakfast Recipes

Lunch Recipes

Snacks

Dinner

Treats

Drinks

So what are the poor parents to do?

Enter *The Sneaky Chef.*

When I first heard about the concept, I was rather skeptical. Is another cookbook really what everybody needs? I was even philosophically against the idea of trying to "sneak" the right foods, as opposed to teaching children what is "right." After all, my parents never gave me the option of choosing my food ("mom cooks what is good and this is what you eat" had been the guiding principle of my generation). If it worked for me, why should I do it differently with my kids?

On the other hand, I knew too well (both as a doctor and as a parent) that giving the right advice does not guarantee that it's going to be followed. In my role as a physician, I am fully aware of the significant role that good nutrition plays in fighting and recovering from serious illness—as well as of the negative effect of poor nutrition (often the result of eating too much of the wrong things rather than not eating at all) on children's health. Although pediatricians spend a great deal of time emphasizing to parents how important proper nutrition is, we often offer little help on *how* to do it. Thus, despite

my reservations, I tried to keep an open mind about the concept of *The Sneaky Chef.* Over the long months of this book's evolution, I had the chance to observe the care and work that went into it (there is nothing more difficult than trying to create "simple" solutions) and most importantly I witnessed its *effectiveness.* I was truly amazed when I saw how a tray of seemingly "normal" brownies containing secret quantities of fruits, vegetables, and whole grains, was quickly devoured by a diverse group of certified picky eaters (including my own kids!) All of a sudden the "concept" had potential beyond our family's dinner table.

So, what is *The Sneaky Chef?*

Is it a gimmick?

No. It offers creative recipes for really healthy food that anyone can prepare...and that kids actually enjoy eating!

Does it require countless hours in the kitchen?

Admittedly, most recipes require more time to prepare than unwrapping a frozen TV dinner or ordering pizza. However, no mother or father is expected to quit his/her job or interrupt regular daily activities in order to cook. Most *Sneaky Chef* recipes have a preparation time of about 10-15 minutes.

Is it sending the wrong message to the parents and especially to the kids by rewarding picky behavior?

Well, like beauty, messages are in the eye (or rather in the mind) of the beholder. What *The Sneaky Chef* promotes is not the idea that children should eat only what they like. Rather, it offers a pragmatic way to enrich their culinary experiences by bypassing their own negative perceptions Eventually, they may be persuaded to actually try the food without disguises... (exactly the way their parents did when they were children!). With any luck, they may even like it...

Anastassios Koumbourlis, M.D., M.P.H.
Associate Professor of Clinical Pediatrics
Albert Einstein College of Medicine
Chief, Pediatric Pulmonary Medicine
Schneider Children's Hospital

CHAPTER ONE

Keep 'em Happy and Healthy

"On the subject of spinach: divide into little piles.

Rearrange again into new piles. After five or six

maneuvers, sit back and say you are full."

Delia Ephron, —How to Eat Like a Child

It *must have been something I did right,* I thought to myself proudly. Here I had this great eater. We liked to call Emily "Caviar Girl" because caviar is what she wanted as a toddler after having tasted it on New Year's Eve. Pretty unusual for a child that age. But then we never had any problems with her; we could put a variety of foods on her plate and she would eat them all. This is a kid who out-ate me at Japanese restaurants when she was eighteen months old, chowing down on seaweed salad, grilled salmon, boiled soybeans, asparagus spears, and tofu as fast as she could maneuver the chopsticks to deposit the food into her mouth. You name it, our Emily ate it and loved it. It was so easy. I couldn't fathom why everyone seemed to make such a fuss over the whole food thing.

Then we were blessed with another healthy baby girl. It was the same family, same mother, same parenting habits. I applied the same set of healthy principles to this new bundle of joy. Why, then, did little Samantha, from birth, have such an aversion to lumpy foods and an overactive gag reflex? Until she was two years old, she couldn't swallow anything that wasn't entirely smooth. Still, it wasn't so bad; she did gobble up anything mushy, such as avocado, applesauce, mashed sweet potatoes, and mashed sardines. And she loved to eat as much as her sister. I prided myself on having bred yet another "good eater." Cross that off my list of worries.

Just when I thought it was safe . . .

Sammy turned two and a half (the "half" is important, trust me). Suddenly it wasn't so easy to get her to eat what I wanted her to. *Wait a minute*, I thought, *we don't have picky eaters in this family.* At first I chalked it up to the "terrible twos," when toddlers first start to assert some independence. I was sure it must be a passing phase. For the time being, I would just let her have her favorites so that she could keep up her caloric intake.

Fast forward two years, and the phase never passed. It only went downhill from there. I was truly humbled.

And to top it off, I found out that this picky phase was contagious. Emily soon started imitating her younger sister. I had always been teased within my social group for being neurotic about feeding my kids the world's best nutrients to fortify their growing bodies. Now I was exploding with guilt because it didn't work and I was exhausted from trying. No amount of education, career experience, or trips to the pediatrician helped me outwit their stubbornness at mealtime. I read all of the parenting books on picky eaters and tried every trick I heard about. Most of them suggested making the food look cute: asparagus log cabins, or a face with spaghetti hair, meatball eyes, and green bean eyebrows. Cookie cutters are big in this philosophy, as is anything "mini." But I wasn't an artist and cute didn't work. They just targeted what they liked and ate around the healthy stuff.

Mother: "It's broccoli, dear."

Child: "I say it's spinach,

and I say to hell with it."

—*E.B. White, cartoon caption in* The New Yorker

The next tactic was making cooking a family activity. Studies show that the more involved kids are in the shopping, preparation, and cooking of foods, the more likely it is that they will eat it when it's on their plate. This philosophy does have its benefits: The kids have fun, cooking provides quality family time, and to some degree it gets them

to eat. But I was a working mother. I had neither the time nor the patience to keep up that pace.

The whole dilemma really got to me the day I turned on *Sesame Street* and saw that Cookie Monster—whose *raison d'etre* was eating cookies—was now singing about them as a "sometimes food." PBS was handing me yet another reason why it was critical for my children to stop adhering to the typical American kid fare.

I went to a dietician who told me to just keep exposing them to the right foods and eventually they would respond. "It takes a minimum of ten to fifteen exposures before they will willingly eat it," she said. I introduced a new vegetable every week and prepared it differently each day. Whenever I was ready to give up, I remembered the nutritionist's words: "Persistence is the key to success." After a few months, my patience was stretched to the limit. I now knew a dozen ways to serve cauliflower, yet my picky little eaters didn't touch a bite of it.

I had already learned the importance of leading by example, not by words. Researchers at the University of Tennessee concluded that there was a "strong relationship between what foods the toddlers liked and what foods other family members also liked." I was a strong practitioner of this theory in my home. (For instance, I regularly did push-ups in front of my husband to encourage him to do the same!) And since I was a fervent believer in eating nutritiously myself, it was no problem doing it around the kids. Over and over, monkey see, monkey do. Unfortunately, my monkeys didn't . . . and I gained a few pounds.

Of course, all during this period I was also doing the same things other parents do: begging, pleading, threatening, and bribing. The *bite-for-bite* rule became a norm in our house. (Even though experts told me this sends the wrong message. The child thinks, "If they're bribing me to eat this, it must really be bad.")

I knew what the gurus of nutrition had to say about a healthy kid's diet. Unfortunately white bread and macaroni, which were the only things Sammy would eat, were not on their lists. One night, my brother (a.k.a. "Uncle Ninny," the vegetarian of the family) was coming to dinner. I was determined to impress him with how well I fed my kids. I set out for Whole Foods, which had just opened nearby, and loaded my cart with an array of fruits and vegetables and a beautiful piece of salmon for dinner. "All for a good cause," was the mantra I repeated as I fell into a trance chopping the red, then the yellow peppers, asparagus tips, and summer squash for the pasta primavera. I even used whole wheat linguine to fit the whole grains into the meal. Amidst that rainbow of beautiful vegetables, I was sure the kids would hardly notice the brown color or the lovely chiffonade of basil.

We took our seats around the table. I was being, I found out, naively optimistic. When Samantha looked at the platters of food and asked, "What are *we* having for dinner?" I replied sweetly, "This is it, honey. Just one meal from now on for the whole family. Mommy's tired of making three different meals every night. Look at all those pretty colors in the pasta primavera. Pretend you're at an Italian parade — doesn't the basil look like confetti?"

I was selling — no doubt about it.

"Yuck," screeched Emily, still the better eater. "I hate basil (she's never had it, by the way). And it's touching the pasta! I'm not eating anything in *that* bowl."

"Yeah," chimed in her little sister. "Ick! I'm not eating that either. I want bowtie noodles with butter in my Elmo bowl."

My brother shot me a look across the table as if to say, "You're going to put up with that from these pipsqueaks? Just *make* them eat it." If only it were that easy.

Even though I knew that my brother couldn't possibly understand my dilemma—he had no kids of his own—I was embarrassed. I could not get my kids to cooperate on a seemingly simple issue. Reluctantly, I offered to rinse the linguine to rid it of the dreaded basil and transplant the pasta into the Elmo bowl. "No," they insisted, "it's weird. It's *browwwwwwn*. And it touched the leafy green stuff. We want *new* noodles, Mommy. White ones!"

"Kids," my husband commanded, "eat the salmon at least."

"Eeew, Daddy, it's a *fish*," they squealed together.

He turned and begged me, "Just give them what they want, please, so we can eat in peace."

> *"You can learn many things from children. How much patience you have, for instance."*
>
> —*Franklin Jones*

I headed into the kitchen, hungry and tired, and then suddenly caught myself in the act. Slowly I turned, sat down, and glared from one set of big, innocent eyes to the other. With that, I decided I was going to enjoy every last bite of my deliciously healthy dinner — and they could sit back and enjoy the show.

Yet afterwards, I had to acknowledge that I was floundering. I had certainly had conversations with other mothers and knew I was not alone. Still, I was tired of the tricks and the daily fights and cooking three completely different dinners every night. I was worn down by the little-bird chirping from my young ones. Except that unlike chicks in the wild, my little birds weren't squawking for *more* food; they wanted less. I needed a better way. I had to figure out how to play the game better and smarter, and not stay on their level, because you cannot appeal to a child's irrational "logic." After all, I had just seen my two practically fall on the floor crying because one food touched another.

So . . . I couldn't use logic, but I couldn't afford to give up either. Their bodies were continuing to develop whether they were taking in adequate nutrients or not. Somehow I had to outwit them and get them to eat right in spite of themselves.

WHY ARE KIDS SO STUBBORN ABOUT FOOD?

It's all about control. Children can't control much in their young lives, but they *can* call the shots about what goes into their mouths. Any preconceived idea parents-to-be have that they can dictate when, what, and how much their child will eat is doomed from the start. They are no more likely to rule over what goes in their children's mouths than they can control what comes out of their bottoms. Parents who are dead set on forcing their kids to eat, soon find out what those kids are made of: children are capable of responding with an equally intense determination to do the exact opposite of what Mom and Dad ask. They just won't give in no matter what. This is an emotional battle over who's in control, one that parents almost always lose. In many families, the dinner table becomes a battleground and meal time is a power struggle. It is unpleasant for everyone, and it forms an unhealthy relationship with food that lasts a lifetime.

Of course, we all know the nutritional benefits of having your children eat well at a peaceful table, but there are social benefits also. Mealtime is a period that should be fun and should foster bonding among family members. If the focus of the conversation is on coercing the kids to eat what's on their plates, there is little room to ask about the rest of their day or find out how they're doing in school.

I know many people who have very happy childhood memories of time spent around the kitchen table. As author Rachel Naomi Remen describes in her book, *Kitchen*

Table Wisdom, "Sitting around the table telling stories is not just a way of passing time. It is the way wisdom gets passed along. The stuff that helps us live a life worth remembering." Who wants to remember mealtime as an endless fight forcing them to eat their spinach? As parents, we should be using that time to get to know our kids better and find out what's going on in their lives.

"I do not like broccoli.

And I haven't liked it since

I was a little kid and my

mother made me eat it. And

I'm President of the United

States and I'm not going to

eat any more broccoli."

—*George H. W. Bush*

The first step toward creating peace is to understand the "enemy." What are the main reasons for our kids being picky eaters?

- The food looks "weird."
- Kids are naturally averse to foods that are new just because they're new and for no other reason (a phenomenon called "neophobia").
- They're imitating their friends. If friends won't eat it, neither will they.
- They're influenced — and to some extent "brainwashed" — by TV commercials to want only overly-processed junk foods.
- They're extremely sensitive to unusual or new textures (the Ick! factor).

EATING IN AMERICA

What happens to our picky eaters when the foods they're picking aren't in their best interests? They become overfed, yet undernourished, and the number of people in this country who fit that description is staggering. Studies show, and experts point to, the growing number of Americans who suffer from obesity and food-related health problems.

Once we began to realize that it isn't just adults, but children, who are ballooning up, it is especially disturbing. American children are not starving—they do consume large quantities of food—yet many are malnourished because they aren't eating enough of the "right" kinds of foods. For example, the American Dietetics Association reports that 50 percent of all kids ages two through eighteen eat less than one serving of fruit per day.

It is difficult to change this trend because to do so, we would have to introduce children to new foods and steer them away from the stuff that comes in a box, a frozen container, or a plastic bag. Children, unfortunately, are naturally "new-food-phobic." It takes numerous exposures to convince them to try something they haven't had before. Who has that kind of time or tenacity? Today's kids are predominantly eating from the top of the USDA Food Pyramid — fats, oils, and sweets. We need to get them to eat from the healthy groups at the bottom.

The rising rates of childhood obesity are credited with a corresponding rise of health problems found in children — higher cholesterol, Type 2 diabetes, asthma, and others. New studies have even started to link mood and attention disorders with the lack of proper nutrition, contributing to the rise in ADHD, depression, and anxiety. Doctors now have to treat weight and nutrition-related illnesses in children that used to be seen only in adults. Do you want your kids to be among the nine million children who are overweight or obese? Children have enough to deal with when they're growing up without being saddled with a whole host of additional problems.

"Every man is the builder of a temple called his body."

— Henry David Thoreau

Contrast the drawbacks of the typical American diet to the benefits of one that is truly healthy. We are what we eat (literally) so when you feed your children a nutritious diet, you are giving them the building blocks that turn into their growing bodies over a lifetime. Some of the specific benefits of getting your kids to eat better include:

- more energy
- greater physical well-being
- improved mood
- strengthened immunity
- increased brain power
- enhanced qualities of attention
- reduced risk of obesity and corresponding illnesses
- fewer "everyday" illnesses

There are literally thousands of scientific journal articles describing how essential certain fats are to the brain and its development. The human brain is nearly 60 percent fat, and brain growth is critically dependent on the quality of a child's nutrition. One critical nutrient is DHA, an essential fatty acid, recently added to infant formulas and baby foods. Adequate amounts of DHA have been linked to improved vision, better mood, reduced learning disabilities, and improved attention.

A BETTER WAY

In spite of these facts, which most of us have been exposed to in one way or another, the parents I know end up sticking with the tried and true—white pasta, peanut butter and jelly sandwiches, macaroni and cheese, chicken nuggets, and pizza —only because these foods are generally eaten without a fight.

"Health food may be good for the conscience, but Oreos taste a hell of a lot better."

—*Robert Redford*

I wasn't a doctor or a nutritionist, but I was in the trenches with all of the other moms, and I knew there had to be a better way. The issue of our children's health was too important to give up or to give in.

The "hiding technique" occurred to me one day when Sammy was a toddler. She used to eat all kinds of food as long as I made a smoothie out of them. I noticed that I was already hiding ingredients and hadn't realized it. Hmmm. Maybe there was a trick to all this, a creative way to get my kids to eat more vegetables, beans, whole grains, and fruits. It really dawned on me when I was mixing a teaspoon of liquid penicillin into Emily's chocolate pudding, without her knowing it, to cure her strep throat. If it worked with medicine, why couldn't it work with something else? Why couldn't I hide the healthy foods I wanted my daughters to eat inside the foods they *would* eat? I started experimenting in the kitchen and saw the magic work, and I realized that as long as they couldn't see, smell, or taste anything too different, they would eat whatever I gave them without comment. I began matching up list A—the kid-favorite foods—with list B —the super healthy foods. The result was nothing short of amazing. With a dose of creativity, a guiltless willingness to be a bit sneaky (more about this later), and a certain amount of outside-the-box thinking, I was able to conceal previously rejected foods such as whole grains, beans, vegetables, and fruit in many of my children's meals. Mealtimes would pass without my ever hearing the word "Yuck!"

This measure of creativity had a wondrous result. It got our family eating together in peace, and it gave me the peace of mind to know that my children's bodies were receiving the building blocks to grow strong and healthy. This book is the result of that learning/testing process.

"Sneaking" began as a last resort, but it should have been the first and predominant method all along, because it opened up a whole new world for my family, and it took the stress out of mealtimes. Before, food used to be the primary source of fights; now it was no longer an issue. The idea of sneaking is not entirely original to this book. We've all heard Julie Andrews, in *Mary Poppins,* sing, "Just a spoonful of sugar makes the medicine go down." The concept has been around for a while. What I have done is take the germ of the idea of sneaking food and made it into an art. Using my own kitchen as a testing laboratory, I came up with foolproof techniques for working the most nutrient-rich foods into the main foods that kids are known to shovel in without an argument. (This list was partially compiled by the Center for Science in the Public Interest after reviewing children's menus across the country.)

The Sneaky Chef will teach you the same guerrilla tactics I picked up with the same results. You will learn to camouflage the world's healthiest foods inside of your kids' favorites. In business, guerrilla techniques are defined by experts as "unconventional marketing intended to get maximum results from minimal resources. It is a body of un-conventional ways of pursuing conventional goals." If this can work on business competitors, why shouldn't it work on our children? There are more clever and sophisticated ways to introduce fruit and vegetables into our kids' diets than planting bananas in banana bread or adding veggie toppings to pizza (which they often just pick off anyway). There is a more effective way to regulate what they eat than issuing edicts that don't work or by yelling, coercing, cajoling, imploring, or bribing them.

This book is easy to use and practical. It had to be. I, like many of you out there, was a working parent and determined to keep my busy lifestyle from interfering with the raising of healthy children. I'm not here to tell you what you already know, that your kids aren't eating enough vegetables. I understand your frustration, and I know all the tricks you've tried that either haven't worked at all or only worked at a few mealtimes.

But the book isn't only for your kids. It's for you, too. It is designed to vastly reduce the time and effort you have to invest in your children's diet. You know that feeling at the end of the day, after dinner when you are drained and you can't stand one more argument? Well, this book can't help you figure out how to make your children put their toys away or stop fighting with each other, but it can reduce and eventually eliminate the constant nagging, that goes on at family meals. You deserve a break. The following benefits of this book will help you invest your time and energy more wisely:

• **Make-ahead advantage**—Nearly all of the foods you'll be adding to your kids' meals can be pre-prepared in less time than thirty minutes per week and stored to be used later in recipes.

- **Quick and quicker**—Since time is of the essence for moms, the methods of adding healthy foods into recipes takes less than five minutes, and less than thirty minutes for the "from scratch" options.

- **Easy**—These techniques are incredibly easy and require minimal cooking experience.

- **Processing**—The most common technique used to hide the good stuff is pureeing in a food processor or blender. This is easier and quicker than chopping vegetables by hand, which is the usual technique for preparing healthy food. And the result is that you're providing even more concentrated and nutrient-dense ingredients, so you only have to use small amounts for greater impact.

- **Alternative to pureeing**—If you can't, or don't want to puree, you can use jarred baby food as a convenient alternative for many of the fruits and vegetables you'll be adding to your kids' meals.

- **Saves time and money spent going to the doctor**—Since your kids will be eating more nutritiously, their immune systems will be stronger, and they'll come down with fewer everyday illnesses that require doctors' visits. The time and money you save on just one of these visits will more than pay for a week's worth of pureeing!

- **End of the food wars**—There is no way to measure the amount of time and energy we expend trying to plead with resistant children to eat healthier and the toll that takes on the parent/child relationship. The relief brought by *The Sneaky Chef* will prove invaluable.

CHAPTER TWO

For Their Own Good

Being a "sneaky chef" is simply hiding something from our children for their own good. This is something that we do as parents all of the time to protect them from information they're not old enough or sophisticated enough to handle.

If Great Uncle Buck leaves our children a nice sum of money, do we give it to them to spend on toys today, or do we invest the money wisely for them? We would no sooner ask our kids how to invest their inheritance, than we would ask them to plan the family's meals for a week. Part of unspoken parenting wisdom is that we don't volunteer anything that they're too young to comprehend. When we want our kids to get more exercise so that they're physically fit, we make it fun by playing games and sports, rather than putting them on the treadmill for an hour while lecturing them about obesity and the health benefits of exercise. We frame exercise in terms of fun and play, even though we secretly know our motivation is to keep them healthy and fit. Hiding pureed carrots in a yummy muffin is the equivalent of playing a game of tag with your child; forcing him to eat cauliflower straight up is the equivalent of sticking him on the stationary bike and telling him that if he doesn't keep going, he'll get fat.

"I'M AFRAID OF GETTING CAUGHT"

It is true that clandestinely slipping ingredients into kids' favorite dishes when the kids aren't looking is slightly risky business. It's not as if we can erect an invisible fence around the kitchen and keep them out while we're cooking. They could wander in when we're scooping green puree from the blender into the meatballs. Something about this will arouse their suspicion. "Mommy, what is that green stuff you're putting in the spaghetti?" Fortunately, we can usually think fast and come up with a response. One day I found my youngest had silently walked in and was standing behind me. "What's that wheat germ doing on the counter near my chicken nuggets?" she asked innocently. Momentarily, I was thrown off, but I quickly recovered by feigning shock. "What!! How did that get there! There must be a ghost in the refrigerator. Quick, let's get him before he puts something in your food." We ran around pretending to look for the wicked ghost, and then she skipped out of the kitchen laughing.

Fortunately, kids are easily distracted from a train of thought, particularly if the distraction is funny or interesting. It is also fortunate that they have short attention spans. By dinnertime, my little girl forgot all about the feared wheat germ and happily ate her chicken nuggets without ever knowing about my covert operation to slip the ingredient into her meal. Kids aren't adults. They aren't sophisticated or practiced in the art of deception. Of course, they do fib once in a while, but they usually aren't very good at it. Most adults are adept at lying when they feel they have to, but it is all in the name of good manners. By the time we're old enough to vote, we have learned to convince our girlfriend that we love her new haircut, when in reality, she looks like her head was caught in a cement mixer.

Also working in our favor is the fact that our kids haven't learned to be suspicious yet. Their world is a simple one where they don't know about partisan politics and corporate "creative" bookkeeping. At times, we have to use their gullibility to our advantage. Again, if you think about it, you realize that you do it all the time with a perfectly easy conscience.

"BUT I WANT MY KIDS TO LEARN GOOD HABITS."

One other consideration about being a sneaky chef that must be examined is that if we keep serving our kids food that doesn't seem particularly healthy, how will we train them to adopt a healthy diet as they grow up? Won't they just go right on eating their favorite foods when we aren't there to cook for them? The problem is that they'll go to Burger King, and the short order cooks in the back won't be sneaking blueberries and spinach into their double bacon cheeseburger. Isn't it part of our job as parents to train our kids to know a good diet from a bad diet?

The answer is yes, but we can't do it in a war zone. If every night at the table we have to be engaged in a running battle over whether they'll touch what's on their plate, who is winning?

It is not my contention that we should be crafty about getting the good stuff into their systems and then never say another word about food. Being a sneaky chef is no substitute for teaching good eating habits and continuing to educate our children about the benefits of smart eating. The problem is that it's difficult to get your kids to listen to you talk to them about health if you're always fighting over what's on their plate. And you cannot be a patient teacher if you're worried over the fact that no matter what you say, the only things your kid wants to eat are pizza and hot dogs. You must have the peace of mind of knowing that you don't have to "win" the argument at this stage of the game. They're too young to understand about nutrition and growing bodies, and too impulsive and undisciplined to force themselves to chow down on something that doesn't taste good just because it's good for them. Parents who feel pressured to get their kids to eat their vegetables "right now," because they're worried that if the children don't, their growing bodies will be deprived of important vitamins and minerals, will push too hard. The result will just be more resistance. The kids will feel defiant and angry, so they won't be in a position to listen openly.

You know this from arguing with adults: When people are fighting, and they're both invested in winning (believe me, children are just as competitive about winning as adults), neither party is in a listening mode. Secretly slipping nutritious ingredients into meals actually facilitates teaching because it takes away the stress and the urgency to win. We know we're getting what we want, even if they don't, so we can guide them in the direction of a healthy diet in a more relaxed atmosphere. Now you can serve small amounts of brown rice and vegetables along with the chicken nuggets and explain to your son how the whole foods will help him make it onto the basketball team more than if he just eats the nuggets alone. Just keep introducing the broccoli in a casual, matter-of-fact way. Eventually, the children will accept it as part of the meal and stop resisting it as an alien food. Kids aren't any different from grown-ups. We all resist being told what to do. Human beings have always been more open to suggestion than to command. Once you know you have gotten the nutrition into their growing bodies, you can afford to be patient and persuade through suggestion.

"I'M NOT GIVING IN WITHOUT A FIGHT."

Whenever we talk about feeding our kids, we're always talking about larger parenting issues at the same time. And the decisions we make about food have to fit in with our overall philosophy about how to discipline kids. Are we the permissive type, the authoritarian type, or something in between? I have heard mothers voice the objection that making a special version of a dish to seduce kids into eating it is coddling them. They ought to just do what we tell them, right? We're in charge; they don't have to like everything we tell them to do, right? Almost anyone who has kids will tell you that it's never that simple. Children aren't dogs; they aren't bred to be obedient. And even before they can talk, they already have opinions.

In general, it is true that overly permissive parents who let their kids run the ship end up producing self-absorbed brats who never grow out of the "me first" stage of childhood. They treat everyone they meet as if they are their mother, the mother who waited on them hand and foot. They're still stuck in a type of behavior that demands immediate gratification. If they don't learn to delay gratification sometimes, or to learn to do what they *should* rather than what they *want,* then as adults they will continue to be impulsive and selfish. Whenever they're hungry, they'll gravitate toward the comfort foods that taste good but provide little in the way of nourishment. They won't have taught themselves to make wise choices instead of self-indulgent choices. Rest assured. Using *The Sneaky Chef* method includes educating them about the value of healthy food.

We've all heard the phrase, "Learn to pick your battles." With kids, the one area where you are unlikely to win a battle is over food. Deciding what to put into their mouths is how they most assert their independence, since they have so little control over the rest of their lives. Whether they can express this idea or not, it is *their* body, and they don't want to be pushed around and told what to put into it. Lord knows, children don't win very often. They are constantly at the beck and call of adults, asked to wait patiently while Dad picks out a buzz saw at the hardware store, asked to hurry up be-

cause Mom is late, asked to be polite when the dinner guests show up, and so on. When you think about it, isn't it reasonable of them to want a little control once in a while, to want something in life to be on their terms?

So what's a mom to do? She cannot wield the kind of absolute power at the dinner table that she does with other issues, such as telling them to go to school, making them put shoes on when it's time to go to a wedding, or insisting that they wear a helmet when riding bikes. All of these are important. "But," you say, "so is food. My kids have growing bodies that need nutrition now. I can't just let this slide."

No, you really can't, but you don't have to win by fighting. At this game, you can win by being clever and creative.

One common question I am asked is whether I ever tell my children that I am sneaking ingredients into their meals, and if I do tell them, do they mind? In general, I don't tell them about all of the ingredients in a dish because if I do, the odds are high that they'll push it away (even if they are in the midst of enjoying it). If I don't reveal my secrets, they'll eat it. It's just that simple. For reasons I cannot begin to understand, when children know something is good for them, they think it can't possibly taste good—even if it really does!

The problem we're dealing with is, again, an age-old parenting dilemma: How can you talk rationally with someone who hasn't reached the age of reason yet? How do you contend with irrational demands that always, in some way at least, represent a real need? They may seem to say no just to annoy you, but kids really do have to learn to say no to adults. Saying no is a simple act that helps them separate from their parents and define themselves as individuals. This is a natural part of the development process. We don't have to stop them from doing this, but we do have to elicit their cooperation sometimes, even if they don't know it. And there are times when we have to let them feel that they have won, too, so they don't grow up feeling powerless.

"Okay," you say, "let them say no once in a while. But do they have to be so irrational about it?" On one day, they'll accept green vegetables without complaint. On the next, they'll make a face that suggests you're serving them garbage. Their mind seems to be telling them *not* to like the food.

Although this might not make sense to you, it does no good to try to dismiss their objections and force them to do what you want. You have to work with the psychology of a child. All mothers know that the habit of saying no, just for the sake of saying it, doesn't end with the terrible twos. Kids go on putting up resistance to what their parents want, right into their teenage years. This is their way—albeit sometimes misguided— of establishing autonomy. We have to find various ways of dealing with that tendency. Sometimes it involves challenging them outright and sometimes it calls for outsmarting them and avoiding a confrontation altogether.

If you are a sneaky chef, you are being somewhat misleading, but it is a form of loving deceit. I am simply teaching you to "package" the foods you give your children in much the same spirit that the food companies do. There is a reason that breakfast cereal comes in the form of cute barnyard animals or colorful letters of the alphabet. The marketing departments recognized the importance of making their products child-centered. They came down to the kids' level to make their food appeal to them. When you stop to think about it, you do this all the time. You play board games that your kids can compete at on their own level. You change the level of language you use when talking to them and choose words they can understand. Now you are simply doing the same with food.

You have nothing to worry about if you work with the philosophy and methods in this book. If you have ever told your kids there is a tooth fairy, or told them they have nothing to worry about (when there actually was) just to protect them, or you gave them a simplistic explanation for something be-cause the real reason was too complex —then you already understand that omitting a few details once in a while is not out of order. The result is a double victory for families— parents get their kids to eat healthier without the battle, and kids get what they want from parents.

My Philosophy about Food

"You are what you eat."

—American proverb

In the old days, to shop at a natural food market, I had to squeeze down the aisles of a tiny, dusty little shop that was filled with moldy granola, shriveled plums, rotting bananas, and swarming fruit flies. Years later, I discovered the natural superfood store, Whole Foods—a mecca for fresh, beautiful vegetables and fruit with a dizzying array of choices.

The first time I visited the store, I strolled down the aisles and was awestruck at the cornucopia of colors. Venetian red tomatoes, sea-green celery, red, yellow, and green bell peppers. As I stood in front of the display of organic peppers, I found myself in a sort of trance. I was startled out of it by a man who came up behind me. After a moment he said, "I only wish my wife would look at me the way you look at those vegetables!"

I know I am gushing, but I do love good food. That doesn't mean it has to be fancy, expensive, or complicated to prepare. In fact, sometimes the simpler it is, the better. There is nothing more delicious than a ripe, golden peach or a vibrant red, vine-ripened tomato in the summer, or a sweet purple grape. One day, I almost made myself sick eating a bucket of dark red, sweet cherries, off a tree on my brother's organic farm. I sat on the ground under that tree and thought happily, you can just bury me here, my life is complete. I am the kind of person who cannot fathom it when someone says they forgot to eat lunch. That's like saying you forgot to cash in a lottery ticket. I think the last time I skipped a meal was when I was giving birth. I waited till it was over, but soon after I ordered the finest BLT on rye — with fries. I deserved it!

TWO SCHOOLS OF THOUGHT

There are two schools of thought about food:
One, Food is pleasure.
Two, Food is medicine.

From the story I just recounted, you might think I'm in the first camp. However, when I played for my college tennis team, I truly found out just how "medicinal" food really is, in other words, the direct impact it has on the body. To become a peak performer, I conducted a great deal of personal research on how different foods affected my game. I ended up choosing nutrient-dense foods that would sustain high energy levels and strength during practice and matches. The last thing athletes want to go through is crashing and burning, or feeling shaky before a match is over. The results of this research have stayed with me all of my life and found their way into the pages of this book. This is information that mothers really need because studies show that children at play actually use more energy than most athletes.

Once the intense demands of the college tennis tour ended, I wandered back into the food-as-pleasure school. My career path shifted when, after I graduated, I had the good fortune to land a job at the epicurean powerhouse, *Gourmet Magazine*, which epitomizes the pleasure concept. Every recipe that appeared in an issue celebrated the taste-is-king philosophy.

Up until then, the only exotic food I ever ate was in a restaurant or in someone's home. But in *Gourmet's* private dining room, I got to eat five-star meals and test amazing recipes. However, I wasn't much of a cook myself. I soon realized, though, that I had better get serious about it. Even though I was on the business side of the magazine, it was a job requirement to cook at least one recipe from the current issue every month. Then I would have to discuss the results in a public forum, so I had to make sure I knew what I was talking about. This was the world's best training ground for making food look and taste good. Besides, I had just gotten married, and at least one of us had to learn to cook so we wouldn't have to resort to takeout every night!

My experience at *Gourmet* prompted me, over the next few years, to enroll in cooking classes at culinary institutes. In addition to learning proper cooking skills, I developed a subtle appreciation for how flavors blend together and found out how to employ more advanced techniques. In the ensuing years, as my interest grew, I took more and more cooking classes and ultimately became certified in the master techniques of healthy cooking. I now teach cooking classes at some of these very same cooking schools!

If *Gourmet* reinforced the idea that food is pleasure, my next job proposed the notion that it could also be healthful. And more than that — that healthy food could actually taste good. At *Eating Well* magazine, they put a great deal of effort into making food taste good, but there was no question that their main focus was health. I worked in close partnership with cutting-edge leaders in the field of nutrition. These were the people who were talking about the evils of *trans fats* ten years before the food giants ever heard of them. My editors were among the first to publicize *nutraceuticals,* a term coined in the 1990s by Dr. Stephen DeFelice to mean "any substance that is food or a part of a food and provides medical or health benefits, including the prevention and treatment of disease."

Everything these people said made sense to me and threw me back to the time when I had been an athlete and understood the impact food had on my body. It was clear that my days of eating strictly for pleasure were numbered. The shift was not as difficult for me as it was for some, because the philosophy did align with my background and my growing belief that food was one of the best ways to preserve good health and prevent illness.

"Leave your drugs in the chemist's pot if you can heal the patient with food."

—*Hippocrates*

I have always known that food directly affects the way I feel, both immediately and in the long run. Many studies have shown this correlation, yet no fact is more convincing than when you experience a clear connection in your own body between the way you eat and your energy levels, the strength of your resistance to everyday illness, your moods, and even to your ability to think clearly. I have seen this correlation, not only in myself, but in others. My mother is a beautiful, active woman who has always eaten healthy food and is the only one of her friends who doesn't take a single prescription medication or spend her days shuttling to doctors. She lives a fuller and more vibrant life than anyone her age. For me, she's a living example of the adage, "An ounce of prevention is worth a pound of cure."

We are living in a time when there is a media explosion about the health benefits of certain foods, popularly called "superfoods" or "medifoods," which contain antioxidants and phytochemicals. The focus is on using food items themselves as health supplements rather than taking a supplement in pill form. In other words, the nutrition in food is considered a better disease fighter than anything that can be made up in a lab. Today, you can't open a magazine or newspaper without coming across information about antioxidants and phytochemicals, which are found in blueberries, pomegranates, broccoli, oats, beans, salmon, soybeans, tea, and even chocolate. All of these and more are being touted for their ability to stave off disease and increase longevity.

"Let food be thy medicine,

thy medicine shall

be thy food."

—*Hippocrates*

In this book, you will find virtually all of these foods as secret ingredients so that they can be incorporated into your family's diet on a daily basis. Bite for bite, calorie for calorie, these superfoods pack in more nutrition than anything else you can eat. All of the make-ahead purees use cauliflower, zucchini, peas, spinach, broccoli, yams, carrots, or white beans.

The methods I present here represent my effort to make peace between the two camps of food-as-medicine and food-as-pleasure. I don't believe they have to be mutually exclusive. Why can't we have our cake and eat it too? This is an especially important attitude to take when feeding children, because they don't buy into the food-as-medicine idea. You cannot convince a child that he should like what's on his plate simply because it's good for him. He doesn't care. He wants to enjoy his meal. Adults may be able to conceptualize the need to make certain food choices in favor of longer-term health goals, but our kids are not that mature. They cannot see the bigger picture. You can't tell a child that when he's fifty, he'll be glad he ate his broccoli today because he has no concept of himself reaching fifty. Only aliens are fifty!

Kids live in the present. They see only as far as this meal, and they want it to taste good. This is one of the main reasons we must *appear* to satisfy their need for immediate gratification — to get them to eat right whether they're convinced of the reasons for it or not.

FOOD IS A MANY SPLENDORED THING

We all know that food is a lot more than medicine *or* gratification. From our first moments of life, it takes on a meaning far beyond mere sustenance. In general, the provision of food by parents forms a familial bond that lasts a lifetime. Cooking for someone is such a profound act of giving, and this means for anyone. The pleasure we get from feeding others often seems rooted in our maternal instincts to nurture our offspring. When we thoughtfully prepare a delicious meal for friends or family, it not only makes the recipient feel loved, but it fills our hearts as well. Food is one of the most profound joys and pleasures of human life. For me, there is nothing more gratifying than planning, shopping for, and preparing a loved one's favorite dish and watching the pleasure they get from devouring it.

The whole concept of food has far-reaching effects on all of society. Historically, to "break bread" with someone refers to a social meeting, but one in which food is served. Sharing a common meal is one of the most universal ways of creating social bonding, even between enemies. When people sit at a table and break bread together, it immediately establishes a tone of cooperation. We incorporate food into almost all social acts. Why, for instance, do we instinctively lay out a few dishes of hors d'oeuvres when guests arrive? Why not play a game of checkers instead? Why not just sit and talk without any food or drink? Because food is the universal language of friendliness and hospitality. Offering something to eat says, "You are welcome here." Eating is the one thing we all have in common, even if we don't always agree on what we want to eat.

Meals also create some of the most prominent memories of our childhood. The nightly dinner table is the place where we share what happened during our day and sometimes have lively "discussions" about religion, politics and movies. A table of food is always laid out at extended family gatherings, and something memorable usually occurs. Uncle Larry says the wrong thing. Aunt Jeanie announces she's getting married again. The baby spits up in Grandma's hair. Name a single celebration that we don't mark with food, or with a particular type of food. Easter is ham, Thanksgiving is turkey, and so on. Celebrations and food are practically synonymous. And yet so are the sad times. After a funeral, everyone shows up with plates of food, perhaps as a symbol that life goes on.

All of this makes the kitchen a very important place. In many households, the kitchen is the most used room in the home. Whenever there is a party or a big dinner, everyone gathers in the kitchen until the meal is served. Generations of a family gather together to help create a meal, often passing down years of history through family recipes. The luscious smells from the oven fill the house. Later in life, we may not always remember the details of that day, but we will often remember the smells. Something about the sense of smell can bring us back to a place and time like nothing else. All it takes is a vaguely familiar scent, and we are instantly transported. We always remember the comfort foods and are drawn to them in times of stress. Whatever Mom served us when we felt vulnerable, it is the warmth, safety, and comfort of those foods that rekindle those feelings in us later.

TAKING AN APPROACH THAT WORKS

Because food can be such a favorable force in our lives, my approach to it tends to be positive, not negative. Much of the health news in the media today is aimed at the aging baby boom population, at how we treat our own bodies and those of our children. They cite the latest health scares and offer us new ways to prevent disease and not die prematurely of stroke or heart attack or cancer. Some food group is always labeled bad, and we're told we must immediately banish it from our diet. Of course, they also identify the food items we should eat more of, but it's still in the context of what to fear and avoid. Either way, these scare tactics take a negative slant and play on our fears.

"A food is not necessarily essential just because your child hates it."

—*Katherine Whitehorn*

Today cancer, high cholesterol, heart disease, diabetes, and high blood pressure top the charts of conditions to be afraid of. I am not saying that as adults, we don't need to pay attention to them and act accordingly. I am simply saying that the concerns that are appropriate to address for the aging population are not appropriate for our children, who won't be faced with these medical issues for years.

> *"Let food be thy medicine, thy medicine shall be thy food."*
>
> —*Hippocrates*

Instead, I take a more positive approach to feeding children. I focus almost solely on *nutrition enhancement*. I choose foods that boost brain power so that they do well in school, that stabilize energy levels so that they can play till they drop, that build strength and immunity so they feel healthy and happy. Unlike other books that warn us to remove entire food groups from our kids' diet, *The Sneaky Chef* is an advocate for all the foods that should be *added*.

We all know the basics. Kids eat too much refined sugar, saturated fat, and processed foods, and I have reduced all of these in my book to the extent that it's possi-

ble. But we have to deal with reality here. The reason we're talking about these foods at all is because our kids like them. If we do have to serve them in some small amount, let's do it without guilt, and let's take a breather from what's bad and talk a little less about forbidding things. After all, what is "forbidden fruit"? It is the very thing that becomes the most desired. I would much rather focus on how to enhance a meal. You won't get a guilt trip from me that you're not feeding your kids enough vegetables; instead, you will get a simple solution.

I must add here that I use this same approach when it comes to setting limits with my kids. Today, there is a great deal of concern, and rightly so, about the influences our youth are being exposed to. When I hear my daughter repeating lines from certain songs, it makes me cringe sometimes. Does she even know what they mean? Parents do have to exert control over incoming information from the media and over their children's activities. We also have to put our stamp on what they eat; otherwise, we'll all have overweight, unhappy kids. And yet parental control does not have to come in the form of a constant battle. Like any good general commanding the troops, we have to engage in strategic planning if we want to ensure victory. The troops, our kids, don't have to be involved in every detail.

One ace in our hand in getting our kids to do what's right is that they have an innate desire to please us. They actually thrive on parental approval, so even though they're arguing with you over dinner, they are conflicted about it. They want what they want, and often they're just fighting to get us to approve of it. That's why the sneaky methods work; they keep us from having to berate our kids every time a cookie touches their lips. We need to remove the condemnation and guilt and let them win sometimes.

As you can see, I believe that encouraging and guiding kids works better than dictating. Throughout the course of their childhoods, you will find yourself arguing with your children over a number of issues. Food is the one power struggle where you'll have the least control. You could win, of course, using draconian measures, but what would the cost be? An authoritative, dictatorial approach may get your children to eat a few bites of extra vegetables, but their willingness to eat them will not last beyond your control. How many of us

now love the very food we were forced to gulp down as children?

"Be not angry that you cannot make others as you wish them to be since you cannot make yourself as you wish to be."

— *Thomas à Kempis*

Forcing a person to eat something, will cause her to hate it — plain and simple. And forcing her to finish everything on her plate will create an unhealthy over-eater. In a 2006 study done at Boston University, it was concluded that parents who use rigid discipline with their children over food are five times more likely to raise obese children. Using the authoritative "clean your plate, or else!" approach can work a little too well — it can teach kids to eat whether they're hungry or not just because food is on their plate. This ends up becoming a lifelong habit, eating for any reason other than being hungry, which is a prime contributor to obesity. Kids should be able to stop eating when their brains send the "no longer hungry" signal to their stomachs. (Naturally, you have to discern when your kids aren't hungry for split pea soup, but they're starving for chocolate ice cream. As my kids and their friends always say, "My dinner side of my belly is full, but my dessert side is still hungry.") In my opinion, rewarding a child with words or goodies for being a member of the "clean plate club," or punishing them for not being a member, is a mistake.

"Vegetables are a must

on a diet. I suggest carrot

cake, zucchini bread, and

pumpkin pie."

—*Jim Davis,* Garfield

SEEKING BALANCE

If you make the meal taste good, you won't have to form a "clean plate club." Let's try to balance our children's love of good food with food that is good for them. Establishing balance means you can eat tasty food that's also healthy. I believe that a workable plan, especially for our kids, is to eat everything in moderation. This means that you don't have to cut fat, sugar, and carbohydrates entirely out of anyone's diet. Let's face it, the reason we overindulge in these foods is because they taste good. Life would be unappealing indeed if we cut out pleasurable eating.

Many adults who want to lose weight try this strategy of completely purging foods from their lives. They believe that they can refrain from eating the sinful substances by exercising pure willpower. It might work for a while, but sooner or later, there will be a backlash. The person who won't touch sugar for three months will suddenly eat an entire quart of rocky road ice cream in one sitting. I call this the purge/splurge see-saw. You deprive yourself of everything you want, and then, when there is the tiniest crack in the dam, the floodgates open wide and you give in to every sinful desire. Then comes the guilt and self-loathing.

We can't win this struggle, but we can't afford to lose it either. Where does that leave us?

ADOPTING A WIN/WIN APPROACH

The need to come up with a win/win approach is probably what led you to buy this book in the first place. The whole key to it is to trick the mind out of deprivation mode, which no one can exist in for long. We have to reward ourselves for doing what's right and enjoy life's guilty pleasures once in a while. If we force ourselves to choke down a stinky bowl of steamed cauliflower when we would rather be eating a scrumptious plate of macaroni and cheese, then we will feel deprived. Yet we can't just give in and eat mac and cheese every night and never touch a vegetable. We need to trick our minds into thinking we're eating sinful foods, when in reality we are consuming something with all of the nutritional benefits of a bowl of vegetables.

Every recipe in this book is dedicated to making healthy foods taste decadent. To be brutally honest, it is to make healthy food look sort of *unhealthy*. If we know we have to make vegetables part of our diet, but we force ourselves to eat ones we don't like without any disguise, we will feel deprived and go right on craving all the wrong foods. Why not eat the mac and cheese, but boost it with cauliflower puree? Then we can have our cake and eat it too. When there is the added component of trying to eat healthy *and* trying to lose weight, then you may have to tweak these recipes a little more. What you don't want to do is banish mac and cheese from your life if it is a dish you love. Again, the principle is to strike a balance by making healthy foods satisfy your sense of taste. This may sound like cheating, but what's wrong with cheating if it works? I have struggled for most of my life to balance my love of eating with my desire to be thin. The most successful weight-loss diets are the ones that let you eat at least some of your favorite foods without feelings of deprivation. That's why they put decadent-looking cheesecakes on the cover of the diet magazines. We're trying to find a way to eat seemingly sinful foods and still lose weight.

With the sneaky chef method, we're doing something like this for our children. Why should healthy food feel like a punishment? Simply by making the food look friendly and familiar, we can achieve our own goals and make them happy at the same time. Spinach doesn't have to look like something that was dug out of the bottom of a bog. In one of my recipes, it is hidden in creamy chocolate pudding!

Life itself should be fun and delicious and not so serious. But it won't be fun for long if we are destroying our health. I say we can win at both games.

NO EXTREMES – MODERATION

We cannot keep our kids tethered to our belts. They have to leave home some time, and when they do, they will eat cotton candy and greasy French fries on occasion. Even if they don't like cotton candy, if they're at Six Flags with their friends who are eating it, they're going to pretend they like it. They're the ones who have to fit into that world, and I don't want to make it any harder than it has to be.

"Pick battles big enough to matter, small enough to win."

— *Jonathan Kozol, On Being a Teacher*

Living by the 80/20 rule is my goal. Twenty percent of the time, I give in to the prevailing conditions and let go of the ideal. Only recently, I gave in to my kids' demands to make their lunch sandwiches with white bread because all of the other children have it. I made this choice knowing that this would get them to eat the protein-rich turkey on the inside and keep them from tossing the entire sandwich made with whole wheat. I decided that I would compensate for the missing fiber at another meal in some sneaky way. Since I am known as the mother who is writing a healthy cookbook for kids, this could have been a source of embarrassment for me, but I put my own needs behind me so that the kids could feel "normal."

Moderate parenting creates children who don't go to extremes for the sake of rebellion. I have seen too many adults addicted to sweets as a direct result of an overly strict upbringing. If you want your children to crave something, just forbid it outright. No food is forbidden in my house; it's just not allowed on a daily basis. It shocks my kids when, on rare occasion, I bring home a box of Ding Dongs, but my approach is successful because they don't covet the outlawed treat incessantly. My dear friend Abby has beautiful clear glass jars of candy sitting right on the kitchen counter, stuffed with a rainbow of colors. Her pantry looks like the world's best-stocked snack machine. Yet her kids barely notice any of it and rarely eat it. Her style may not work in every household, but there is something to be said for this kind of availability of forbidden fruit; it takes the power from it. We all tend to want what we can't have.

THE GOOD PARENT FEELING

Here I have presented my innermost beliefs about food. Some you will agree with, some you won't. The question is, how will you use the methods in this book for your own family and how will it make you feel when you do? It has made me feel alternately relieved, clever, creative, accomplished, and empowered. Watching my kids eat veggies, whole grains, legumes, and fruit on a daily basis, makes me feel like a good mother. And the best part is, I no longer have to struggle to get them to do it. This has brought peace to our family table, along with the satisfaction of knowing that I'm giving my kids' bodies the nutrients they need to live happy, healthy lives.

The Lists

If you want to eat smart, you have to buy smart. This begins with making an informed choice and selecting for quality. Sometimes, what's *not* in the food is just as important as what *is* in it. For example, it is critical, when buying for kids, to try to find products that are minimally processed and free of pesticides, antibiotics, and hormones.

Shopping judiciously isn't always easy, but it's worth the extra effort. I want to reiterate what I said in the previous chapter about moderation. We can't always make perfect choices, especially for those who live in regions that don't cater to the health conscious. We can, however, do the best we can do given the possibilities open to us. But wherever you live, you have to be armed with information and resources to put healthy meals on the table.

The following lists cover a wide range of territory: the most contaminated produce, the least contaminated, foods kids most like and dislike, and the staples you will need to have on hand for the recipes in this book.

THE TWELVE MOST IMPORTANT FOODS TO BUY ORGANIC:

Sometimes referred to as "the dirty dozen," the following fruits and vegetables have been found by the USDA Pesticide Data Program to be the *most* contaminated with pesticide residues. Therefore, they warrant buying organic whenever possible. You will notice that most items on the list below have either thin skin or no skin, which is the reason they are exposed to more pesticides that the customer ends up ingesting. If you eat these foods on a regular basis, you are exposing yourself to more than twenty different pesticides per day. They are cataloged from the *most to least* contaminated:

Peaches

Strawberries

Apples

Spinach

Nectarines

Celery

Pears

Cherries

Potatoes

Sweet bell peppers

Raspberries

Imported grapes

THE TWELVE LEAST CONTAMINATED FOODS:

One other way to reduce the impact of pesticides is by stocking up on the foods in this list, which represents the USDA's "least contaminated." In addition, you can further reduce the amount of pesticides by remembering to thoroughly wash (and to peel when it's appropriate) fruits and vegetables. Both of these have been shown to remove detectable residues. Eating from this list exposes us to only about two types of pesticide per day. As you peruse it, you'll notice that most of these items have thick skins (or natural casings) that you don't eat—such as corn husks, pineapple skins, avocado shells, pea pods, onion skins, and banana peels—which protect them from sprayed pesticides. They are listed from the *least to most* contaminated:

Sweet corn

Avocados

Pineapples

Cauliflower

Mangoes

Sweet peas

Asparagus

Onions

Broccoli

Bananas

Kiwis

Papayas

THE "IN" AND "OUT" LISTS WITH KIDS:

If it were up to kids, the world would look like Candyland, and it would be perfectly reasonable to start the day with a few cookies, some gumdrops, and a cold cherry drink. For lunch, they would sit down to a steaming bowl of buttered white noodles, and later an ice cream cone. Let's face it, in American culture today, there are certain foods that most kids love, which I am calling the "In Foods." They are the classic kid favorites, the ones you don't have to argue about. The products with a seriously high "yuck" factor I am calling the "Out Foods." Most kids aren't going to eat them without a fight unless you disguise them. The simple logic behind the recipes in this book is to use the "In" list to conquer the "Out" list.

"IN" (YUMMY)

Gooey candy

Chocolate

Ice cream

White stuff (bread, rice, pasta)

Peanut butter

Cheese, non-smelly (such as American or mozzarella)

Pizza

Pudding

Jell-O

Fried anything (especially potatoes)

Chicken and sometimes shrimp

Ketchup

Hamburgers

Hot dogs

Apple juice

Grape juice

Cookies

Chips

Tuna

Select fruit, such as grapes, apples,
     and bananas

"OUT" (YUCKY)

Most vegetables, especially green

Whole wheat anything

Whole grains, especially brown

Most beans, except maybe "baked"

Most fish, except maybe tuna

Most nuts, except peanuts

Eggs, in almost all forms

Some fruits

STAPLES TO BUY

Keeping in mind the above list, the following is a register of the food staples that I use most consistently in this book. They include many of the yucky foods that are easiest to hide, plus the favorite yummy foods for them to hide in. Keep as many of these as possible on hand and it will be easy to make Sneaky Chef recipes a regular part of your family's daily life. Please keep in mind that you can easily find organic versions of most of these items.

PRODUCE:

Baby spinach

Zucchini, fresh

Broccoli, fresh

Sweet potatoes (or yams)

Cauliflower, fresh

Fresh berries, in season

Bananas

Avocados

Onions

Potatoes, russet

Lemons

MEATS/FISH:

Beef, lean ground

Turkey, lean ground

Hot dogs (no nitrates)

Fish fillets, tilapia or flounder

Chicken, drumsticks and skinless,
     boneless tenders

CEREALS/FLOUR:

Wheat germ, unsweetened

Oat bran

Rolled oats, old-fashioned, not quick cooking

Cereal, high-fiber flakes

Cereal, brown rice

Flour, whole wheat (stone ground)

Flour, white (unbleached)

Flour, whole grain*

Cornmeal

*As an alternative to buying 3 different flours, try Eagle Mills All-Purpose Flour with Ultragrain©

RICE/PASTA:

Brown rice

Macaroni and cheese, boxed (preferably without artificial colors)

Whole wheat pasta, elbows and ziti

Wonton wrappers

Lasagna noodles, "no boil"

BREAD:

Bread, whole wheat

Tortillas, whole wheat flour

Tortillas, corn

Bread crumbs, whole wheat

Whole wheat pita bread, pocketless

Bagels, whole wheat

CANNED GOODS:

Garbanzo beans ("chickpeas")

White beans, ("butter beans," navy, or cannellini)

Refried beans, low fat, vegetarian

Baked beans, vegetarian

Tomatoes, plum, whole

Sardines, in water, skinless and boneless

Tuna, in water (preferably "chunk light")

Tomato paste

Evaporated skim milk

Tomato soup, condensed

JARS/BOTTLES:

Baby foods—especially sweet potatoes, carrots, peas, zucchini, garden vegetables, prunes, plums, apricots, blueberries, spinach, and broccoli.

Pomegranate juice

Salsa

Applesauce

Ranch dressing (no MSG)

Ketchup

Pasta sauce

FROZEN FOODS:

Blueberries, frozen (preferably without added syrup or sweeteners)

Strawberries, frozen (preferably without added syrup or sweeteners)

Cherries, frozen, pitted (preferably without added syrup or sweeteners)

Green peas, sweet

Corn, yellow, off cob

Edamame (soybeans in shell)

NUTS/OILS:

Almonds, blanched and slivered

Extra virgin olive oil, cold pressed

Canola oil, cold pressed

Cooking oil, spray

TEA/COCOA:

Cocoa, unsweetened

Green tea, decaffeinated

DESSERTS:

Chocolate chips, semisweet

Sprinkles, multicolored

Jell-O, not pre-made

Gelatin, unflavored

Chocolate syrup

Whipped cream, spray can

Frozen yogurt, low fat

DAIRY/EGGS:

Yogurt, low-fat, plain

Cheese, low-fat, shredded

American cheese slices

Ricotta cheese, low-fat

Tofu, firm block

Eggs (with added omega-3)

Parmesan cheese, grated

Powdered milk, nonfat

OTHER:

Chicken broth, boxed (no MSG)

Vegetable broth, boxed (no MSG)

Cinnamon

Honey

Pure maple syrup

Pure vanilla extract

Baking powder

Baking soda

Powdered sugar

Brown sugar

Jam, no sugar added

TOOLS:

Parfait "ice cream" glasses

Straws

Popsicle molds

Mini food processor, 3-cup capacity

Mini-bundt ("donut") pan

The Sneaky Chef's Bag of Tricks

"Nothing you do for children is ever wasted. They seem not to

notice us, hovering, averting our eyes, and they seldom offer

thanks, but what we do for them is never wasted."

— *Garrison Keillor*

How do we go about sneaking healthy food into our little ones? The following is a full list of the methods that we will use throughout the book. I have discovered these after years of using my own kitchen as a testing lab and my own children as lab rats. In full faith, I can assure you that these methods really do work. The first one, especially, we will use quite a bit.

PUREE

Pureeing—meaning simply to pulverize food until it is silky in texture—is the most basic and important of all of the tools used by the sneaky chef, mainly because children are naturally drawn to foods of this texture. Possibly it's because pureed food reminds us the most of baby food, and we never really outgrow that.

In this book, pureeing has an added bonus: By changing the appearance and consistency of a food, it makes it easier to hide it in another recipe. My aim has been to find the healthiest products I could puree and then to seek recipes they could be blended into seamlessly. There are many foods that kids won't go near in their virgin condition, but after ten seconds in the blender, those same broccoli stalks they made a face at yesterday are now eaten without a fight. That's because they don't know the puree is hidden in the dish, and you're not going to tell them. You're not lying, you're just not offering information that would only get in their way.

It is an unfortunate fact that modern kids conjure up negative reactions to foods in their natural form. It's almost as if they think they're allergic to nature. Pureeing changes that objectionable natural form so that it becomes unrecognizable, eliminating any protest against a healthy or "new" food. The recognition factor is important because often kids reject food solely on the basis of appearance. They'll say they hate something they've never even had. Once appearance is no longer an obstacle, then you can at least move to the frontier of taste. They will eat whatever is served because now it's familiar, and often they will not notice the slight change in texture or taste.

64   **THE SNEAKY CHEF**

Methods of Pureeing

There are mainly two methods of pureeing.

1. A blender.

A blender not only purees, it liquifies, blends, frappes, chops, and shreds. It is best suited to working with liquids or already mushy solids, but not whole, chopped vegetables. It is also handy for chopping ice. In this book, I recommend it most often for smoothies, ice drinks, and soups.

2. A food processor.

The great advantage of this second method hiding foods is that you have to add very little, if any, water to mash the food into the right consistency. Pureed food should be like mashed potatoes, not like a smoothie. Too much liquid in the mixture, will liquefy the recipe. A can of white beans, which I puree and use often in recipes, requires no more than one or two tablespoons of water to make a smooth bean puree. A head of steamed

cauliflower requires almost no added water since the vegetable contains its own.

For the recipes in this book, I suggest using a small (approximately three-cup) food processor. The larger processors just don't work well unless you insert a large amount of food. If you don't own one now, you might consider purchasing one. I have found KitchenAid's 3-cup Chef's Chopper® Series (you can order on my website) to be the most durable, effective and quietest of all the mini food processors, and it's small enough—and cute enough—to keep handy on the counter. It is also top rated by leading consumer magazines. You will use it quite often for these dishes. You will find, as I have, that it is easier than any other task in the kitchen (such as chopping, for example).

The types of food items you will want to have on hand for pureeing are:

Raw baby spinach

Carrots

Cauliflower

Berries

Onions

Tomatoes

Bread

Legumes (white beans, etc.)

Sweet potatoes

Zucchini

Bananas

Apples

Nuts

Cherries

Tofu

Peas

Broccoli

SPINACH SAFETY: All recipes calling for spinach suggest steaming or boiling fresh or frozen spinach for at least five minutes to eliminate any potential risk of bacterial contamination. Alternatively, chopped frozen collard greens are equally nutritious and mild tasting, and can be substituted in these recipes.

Health Benefits of Method One

Besides the fact that kids won't know they're eating something healthy (and thus fight with you over it), there is another benefit to pureeing: It presents food in a concentrated version so that it is more nutrient dense. Try convincing your kid to eat two whole cups of steamed spinach. You'll be sitting at the table staring him down for a week. If you puree the same amount, however, it comes out to less than half a cup, and that can be added to his spaghetti and meatballs. You use less of it for the same nutritional benefit. And because pureeing puts previously resisted food into a more kid-friendly form, they aren't arguing with you about the type or the amount of the food. The latter is a key point because, as all mothers know, children will not normally eat a large amount of a particular food at one time. They are professional dabblers, you might say. Especially with very young children, a bite of this and a bite of that and they're ready to leave the table. Imagine the satisfaction you'll feel knowing that your child ate an entire cup of broccoli for dinner when previously you couldn't force in a single floret.

Even though fruit is sweet, it is still a challenge coaxing them to eat three to five helpings a day. But try pureeing those blueberries in the blender with vanilla frozen yogurt or ice cream and see how fast she downs that Blue Ribbon Milkshake, which is actually a nutrient-dense powerhouse drink.

Method Two:

COMBINE REFINED AND UNREFINED

Brown vs. white. It may sound like a Supreme Court case, but it's actually a battle between processed and whole grain flour. As healthy as whole grains are, few people today are choosing them for pasta or for bread. Ask for whole wheat pasta at your local Italian restaurant and they'll look at you as if you have two heads. It just doesn't seem to taste as good as its white counter-

part. It certainly isn't the same in the crust of American apple pie or a hot dog bun. We all grew up with white, overly processed products, and it's hard to shake the habit. If you are going to try making a change from anything familiar to something new and unfamiliar, it is always a good idea to make it gradually. This is especially true with children. Kids seek familiarity and they resist change on any level, particularly around food. So if you want to wean them off the white bread and pasta they worship, do it by gradually combining the new with the old. Don't just introduce whole wheat flour one day in everything that is placed on the dinner table and expect them to like it. A severe change away from anything familiar causes resistance in all of us, not just in children. We're used to our cookies and cakes tasting a certain way. Suddenly switching over entirely to whole grain would make them heavy and unpalatable. Using a flour blend lets them retain a good deal of the usual texture and weight while still imparting substantial health benefits, something people are increasingly interested in. When food manufacturers introduce products like Ronzoni's whole wheat pasta blend and Kraft's Chip's Ahoy! (which are now made with whole grains) they reveal their understanding that the public wants taste *and* fiber.

The method for this trick is simple: just create a blend of flours to combine the familiar taste of the refined white flour with the healthier products. Many of the recipes in this book call for a "Flour Blend," which is always **one-third white flour, one-third whole wheat, and one-third wheat germ**. The result is a flour combination that retains many of the properties of the original white flour. People like white flour because it is silkier, lighter, and fluffier. If you use all brown, it will be denser, grainier, and heavier. Modern food products have trained our palates to think the former is just better than the latter. This method gives the food more of the lighter and fluffier consistency of the processed food, which our palate seems to want. It retains the texture, appearance, and some of the taste of the original white flour.

Health Benefits of Method Two

It is extremely important for our kids to fit more whole grains into their diet. When you start making their favorite foods (such as cookies) with this Flour Blend, not only are you accomplishing this, but you are actually training their palate to accept the healthier product. This is a benefit that will last well into their future, helping them develop better eating habits that will last a lifetime. Kids get used to the taste of the less refined new food on a subtle level and aren't even aware of it.

Whole grain products add fiber, which keeps digestion working optimally, adds vitally important vitamins and minerals, antioxidants, and phytochemicals, and reduces exposure to chemically-bleached, altered, and processed foods.

Method Three:
USE FOODS THAT
HIDE WELL

The real secret to being a sneaky chef is, plain and simple, to hide the foods you don't want your kids to know they're eating. Certain foods do this very well, and in this book, some of them might surprise you. For instance, most people are shocked to find that baby spinach has virtually no taste of its own. Consequently, it can be concealed in a great many recipes without anyone ever guessing.

THE FOLLOWING ARE THE BASIC PRINCIPLES OF HIDING FOODS:

1. **Similar colors and textures work well.**

2. **The healthy ingredient has to either enhance the overall original taste or add no taste of its own.**

3. **Sneak means don't taint. You can't** **affect the look or texture of the final product any more than the taste.**

4. **The added ingredient has to be good for you.**

Whatever the product, it must meet three criteria. One, it has to have no real taste of its own. Two, it cannot leave too much of a gritty, leafy, or unusual feel or an off-taste in the mouth that will make it distinguishable from the main dish. (As we will see later, there are ways to deal with these effects if they do appear.) Kids are hyperalert to any differences in their usual foods. In my lab test kitchen, I have also made sure that when these sneaky items are used, there are very few residual flecks of green and no lumpy, grainy, coarse, or harsh texture.

When I tested these products over a period of five years, they had to pass a rigorous test of being bland in taste and virtually invisible in texture. Not only do kids seem to have an unnaturally strong sensitivity to these changes, but they are not in the least bit diplomatic about pointing out their objections. If words aren't derisive enough, they usually make a face. So bland-tasting foods are always chosen over highly pungent ones.

No matter how nutritious something is, it will not work if it changes the taste and texture in an obvious way. It was a sad day when I realized I had to reject beets and asparagus because they have strong tastes that cannot be masked. Happily, I found that seemingly smelly cauliflower, which is very nutritious, was one of the easiest foods to hide when pureed.

The third criterion is that the added ingredient must be similar in color to the main dish. For instance, if you want to hide something in macaroni and cheese, you wouldn't use pureed spinach because it would turn the yellow cheese a sickly color and would impart a "funny" taste. Ideally, the additive will not appreciably change the color of the main dish because that would be an obvious tip-off to kids that you've been sneaky. You have to either match the color of the dish or add a color that doesn't change it. In the above example, you could easily introduce White Bean puree into the mac and cheese because it virtually disappears. For a red pasta sauce, you could stir in pureed orange vegetables.

Drastic changes of color do work if the new color is . . . well . . .pretty. For instance, I have added Green Juice to color frozen vanilla yogurt for a bright green shake for St. Patrick's Day or Earth Day. I have also, as I mentioned earlier, mixed blueberries into ice cream or frozen yogurt for a delicious bright purple shake. I conducted these experiments to take the guesswork out of it for you. So you can be sure that all of the recipes in this book produce acceptable color changes. I have steered clear of any modifications that incite the "Ick!" factor.

If you decide to experiment yourself, it is best to use preschool color-mixing guidelines, which dictate that hues that are opposite each other on the color chart will not combine well. For instance, red plus green equals brown. If you try adding spinach puree to spaghetti sauce, you will end up with a sauce the shade of an old shoe. This only works for pizza if you cleverly hide all of the sauce with cheese. You can add carrots though, because orange doesn't detract from the red. In addition, they cut the acidity of the tomato sauce. Spinach does work well in meat dishes and brownies, though, because brown isn't affected by green.

Please note that certain foods—such as beets and blueberries—have a great deal of natural pigment in them (that's how you can tell they're so healthy) so in many cases, not only are you making the dish look fun, but you are actually adding nutritional value to ice cream, yogurt, and puddings. Some additives, like beets, might add a beautiful hue, but they are unusable because they produce too much of an off-taste and odor. Blueberries, on the other hand, produce a gorgeous purple, yet add a lovely, sweet taste that most children readily accept.

THE MOST COMMON "HIDING" FOODS THAT YOU WILL FIND IN THIS BOOK ARE:

Cauliflower

White beans

Blueberries

Zucchini

Plain yogurt

Raw baby spinach

Peas

Corn

Nuts

Ricotta cheese

Whole wheat flour

Broccoli

Avocado

Olive oil

Sardines

Sweet potatoes

Cherries

Oats

Carrots

Tofu

Green tea

High-fiber cereal flakes

Health Benefits of Method Three

The theory behind foods that hide well in others is: "What you don't know won't hurt you." In this case, it will benefit your children tremendously. They will eat a vegetable they have never tried before instead of rejecting it outright because they *think* it will taste "yucky." Don't forget, kids eat with their eyes as well as their mouths. Hidden items are out of sight, out of mind, into the mouth and the digestive system and forming a healthy body — all without a fight.

Method Four:

SUBSTITUTE NUTRITIOUS LIQUID FOR WATER WHEN BOILING FOODS

This method works best when the food that is being boiled actually absorbs the liquid it is being cooked in. It is not, however, as effective in dishes where the liquid is discarded after the cooking is complete. The exception to this is when the ingredient is fairly porous, like rice, and can absorb some of the nutrients from the healthy liquid.

Any liquid must be chosen not only to enhance the nutritional value of the dish, but also to complement the taste. It cannot contrast or take away from the flavor. For instance, you wouldn't make Jell-O with chicken broth. You could, on the other hand, make Jell-O with blueberry juice. You would not, however, use fruit juice to boil rice. As we will find in this book, though, there *are* some unusual combinations that work very well, that you might not have thought of. For exam-

ple, you can substitute blueberry juice for water when making oatmeal, thereby adding a helping of fruit, as well as a grain, to your kid's breakfast.

The idea behind the nutritious-liquid method is that you don't have to pass up *any* opportunity to sneak nutrition into your children's meals. I'm not saying water is a bad food; it just doesn't add as many vitamins and minerals. By using vegetable broth or milk with canned tomato soup, as opposed to what the label recommends, you contribute extra nourishment and more flavor with no distinguishable off-taste. One liquid to keep in mind, which most parents don't think of giving to children, is decaffeinated green tea, usually considered an adult food. Kids might not drink it by the cup, but you can simmer rice in it (or even make Jell-O with it) and add a ton of nutrition and antioxidants.

Health Benefits of Method Four

As we said, water by itself doesn't add many nutrients to a dish. The following is a list of the nutritional value of the substitutes used in this book:

- Milk adds calcium, vitamin D and protein.
- Blueberry or pomegranate juice adds a concentrated dose of immune-building phytochemicals and a day's worth of vitamin C.
- Green tea provides a significant dose of heart-protecting antioxidants and builds immunity.
- Vegetable broth provides potassium, calcium and all of the essential minerals.
- Chicken or beef broth adds minerals and protein.

BOILED SUBSTANCE	NUTRITIOUS LIQUID
Rice	Chicken or veggie broth, green tea
Jell-O®	Pomegranate or blueberry juice and green tea
Soups	Chicken or veggie broth, green tea
Oatmeal	Milk or blueberry juice
Hot cereal	Milk or blueberry juice
Sauces	Milk or veggie or chicken broth, green tea
Hot cocoa	Milk
Pancakes	Milk
Puddings	Milk
Dumplings	Chicken or veggie broth
Potatoes	Chicken or veggie broth
Pasta	Green tea; chicken or veggie broth

COMBINE FOODS THAT ARE A SPECIFIC NUTRITIONAL COMPLEMENT FOR EACH OTHER

The whole is greater than the sum of its parts. In this case, 1 + 1 = 3. Many of the recipes in this book are designed to combine ingredients that either make a more complete protein or help with the body's absorption of another nutrient.

One reason to find food complements is to form more complete protein. Some plant foods, such as beans or nuts, are incomplete sources of protein by themselves. In combination with whole grains, for example, they form a protein that is equivalent to an animal source. Another important reason to find food complements is that one of the ingredients can help the body to fully utilize a particular nutrient. Magnesium, for instance, is known to increase the body's ability to absorb calcium, so in one recipe we combine magnesium-rich white beans with calcium-rich cheese.

A third reason is to find a way to help the body take in more iron. As parents, we are all interested in making sure our children get enough iron while they are young because this element is essential to growing bodies. Vitamin C greatly enhances the absorption of iron, but in order to work, it must be present in the intestine at the same time as the iron. In other words, kids can't just take a vitamin C tablet after dinner and pray that it works. This is why, in the recipe section, you will see that I include disguised iron-rich spinach in the vitamin C-rich tomato sauce of spaghetti and meatballs.

Health Benefits of Method Five

The combination of ingredients in the recipes in this book has been carefully thought out so that the nutrients commingle to increase their benefits for maximum use in the body. This is what is called a "well-balanced meal." I am certainly not the first person to think of this practice. It is commonly used by nutritionists. The way it

THE FOLLOWING IS A FAIRLY COMPLETE LIST OF THE FOOD COMBINATIONS AND THEIR HEALTH BENEFITS THAT YOU WILL FIND IN THIS BOOK:

Legumes + whole grains

Whole grains + dairy

Legumes + nuts   } Forms complete protein

Legumes + dairy

Meat + tomatoes

Blueberries + spinach

Tomato sauce + beans

Potatoes + white beans   } Enhances absorption of iron

Spinach + tomatoes

Wheat germ + cheese or milk

Ground almonds + milk

Tofu + cheese   } Enhances absorption of calcium

Refried beans + corn tortillas/cheese

Avocado + dairy

works as a sneaky trick is to disguise the combinations in your kids' favorite meals so that even if they will eat only one dish on the table, they will still be consuming a variety of nutrients that bolster each other. Mothers know how common it is for children to dip into only one plate that is served at meal time. This method of combining ingredients in one popular dish ensures that they receive the same benefit as if they were eating from several platters.

Method Six:

IDENTIFY FOODS KIDS ARE LIKELY TO ENJOY STRAIGHT-UP

This is probably the least sneaky of all of my tricks because most mothers have figured out which foods their kids will think of as snacks and not resist. More often than not, they are finger foods of some kind. For reasons child psychologists haven't figured out, children like little foods they can hold in their hand and pop in their mouth. They provide kids with a kind of mini-adventure in the culinary realm. The moment they have to use a knife and fork, it isn't fun anymore. Through experimentation, I have pinpointed a few unusual, yet surprisingly popular, options:

Artichokes, whole

Edamame (soybeans)

Strawberries

Sweet green peas, in shell

Carrots, baby raw

Grapes

Cherries

Pomegranates

Pistachios, in shell

Popcorn

Whole roasted chestnuts, in shell

Snap peas

Corn on the cob

Sunflower seeds, in shell

Chickpeas, roasted crunchy

Please note that I list the pistachios, sunflower seeds, and chestnuts "in shell" to make it not only a fun "activity," but a bit more work for kids to eat. While these are very healthy foods, they are dense in calories which can add up quickly, so the shell slows kids down, and therefore they won't eat as much.

Two conditions absolutely critical to the success of Method Six: One, the kids have to be hungry, and two, there has to be no alternative for them to choose. Given a choice between nachos and snap peas, guess which one they'll pick? By some trick of evolution, the taste of artificial flavors has come to outperform that of natural foods, which are more subtle. If you try serving fresh cherries alongside cherry-flavored snow cones, the unadorned fruit cannot compete. As a result of human interference, junk food has a more intense flavor than nature's product because nature didn't invent its food just to please the tongue.

If your kids aren't already familiar with natural finger foods, experiment by introducing the new type one at a time. Using the process of elimination, try different and new things every few days. Your biggest chance of success occurs when you simply put this new item out on the table before a meal or at snack time when the kids are distracted by playing or watching TV. Another way to trick kids into trying something new is to sit down with a bowl of this strange new thing and enjoy it yourself in full view. Be coy; don't offer them any. Just make sure they see you "privately" enjoying something on your own. A few well-placed "yums" will help too. Other than that, the fewer words spoken about it the better. If they ask, just say it is a special treat or an appetizer. Then let them try this new food and explore it in their own time. Ignore all cries of, "It looks weird! I hate that!" The less of an agenda you have around getting them to eat it, the better the chance that they will.

As I said, this is the least sneaky of all the methods I use. In fact, nothing is actually hidden or disguised about serving foods in their natural, unadorned form. The only con here is that you don't tell them the foods are healthy because we know what a turn-off that is. Labeling them "special treats" makes them sound like junk food, a sure crowd pleaser. Some of the items listed above require a little work on the kids' part, but this only adds to the fun factor. When they peel the leaf petals off an artichoke, one by one, stick them into the dip, and then scrape the tender flesh against the back of their teeth, it teaches them to enjoy a fresh whole food.

Health Benefits of Method Six

Eating whole foods such as fruits, vegetables, beans, nuts, and grains is recommended by nutritionists across the board. There is simply no substitute. In addition, they replace the packaged foods that contain trans fats, artificial colors, and flavors—not to mention copious amounts of sugar and salt—which kids usually eat as snacks. While foods from the earth in their natural state are low in calories, they are loaded with phytochemicals, vitamins, and minerals and they're full of fiber. And in their own way, they are more satisfying, mostly because the fiber provides a feeling of satiation. They leave less room in the stomach for junk food and help stabilize blood sugar levels.

They also take longer to eat on a calorie-by-calorie basis. Eating a whole artichoke takes a good half hour, and the artichoke is high in fiber and fat free. At twenty-five calories, it's a real bargain. Of course, it is also an excellent source of vitamin C, folate, and potassium. Twenty-five calories is equal to about five potato chips, which can be gobbled up in one minute flat and provide nothing but empty calories. Edamame is another good example. Kids love to pop the soybeans—high in fiber and protein, low in carbs, and nutrient-dense—out of the shell and right into their mouths.

These natural finger foods will teach your children healthy eating habits well into their future. They learn that taste doesn't have to come out of a plastic bag or a box.

"It's bizarre that the produce manager is more important to my children's health than the pediatrician."

—*Meryl Streep*

Method Seven:

ALTER THE COOKING METHOD TO AVOID FRYING

Any diet that includes a lot of deep-fried foods places a great deal of strain on the body and increases the risk high cholesterol, heart disease, and obesity. Diets that are high in saturated fat tend to raise bad cholesterol and dangerous triglycerides. Foods that are fried have a lot of saturated fat simply because the fat is cooked right into it. When you fry chicken (with the skin on) in lard, for example, you take something that already contains saturated fat and then add more to it.

But people do love their fried foods, so the sneaky chef finds suitable alternatives. She employs cooking techniques that use as little fat as possible, and when a fat *is* used, she makes sure it is the "good" kind—the monounsaturated oils—that are heart healthy, rather than the saturated fats, or trans fats, that clog the arteries. The sneaky chef chooses to steam, bake, broil, roast, grill, or stir-fry with olive oil instead. And sometimes she cooks food either dry or in broths.

THE MOST COMMON BAKED-NOT-FRIED DISHES THAT WE HAVE FOUND TO BE POPULAR WITH KIDS ARE:

Chicken fingers

Fish sticks

French fries

Tortilla chips

Oven-fried chicken

When you do use monounsaturated oils, it is best to add them at the end of the cooking process so the oil doesn't dry out too fast, which it will do when it is added early. This lets you use much less oil, yet retain all the flavor and benefits of cooking with fat. The visual advantage is the golden luster it leaves and the textural crispiness. Often I recommend misting the dish with olive oil *after* baking it to give it that luminous sheen.

Of course, we should always drain the oil off fried foods on a paper towel after cooking to soak up the excess. Other methods to lower oil intake include:

- Measuring the oil with a teaspoon instead of pouring it right out of the bottle, which often leads to adding more than you want
- Basting it on with a pastry brush, which lets you apply a small amount that evenly coats the food
- Blasting the dish with high heat under the broiler for a minute, which crisps the high fiber breading on many of my recipes
- Using broth, instead of oil, to give a recipe the juiciness it needs to mimic fattier foods

As a mother, I know that kids head straight toward the dishes that are fried and avoid the ones that are steamed or boiled. That is why I have shared recipes that make food look and taste as if it were deep fried, even when it isn't. As with all of the other tricks in this book, no one has to hear about the chef's secrets. Telling kids how the food was really prepared is more than they need to know. All that matters is that they devour the healthier food while believing it's the same thing they'd buy at Burger King.

Health Benefits of Method Seven

This is not a fat-free cookbook. Giving your children the right amount of the heart-healthy oils is just as important as keeping them from eating lard. Adding a little bit of oil to vegetable and bean dishes, for example, helps the body absorb vitamins and antioxidant phytochemicals that are fat soluble. Consuming monounsaturated and nut oils not only keep you from the harmful oils, but they can actually lower cholesterol levels. Some products even impart essential omega-3 oils that elevate moods, protect the heart and brain, and overall are vitally important to achieving optimal health.

Deep frying is probably the most harmful cooking method. My advice is to avoid it at all costs because the saturated and hydrogenated oils that are used for deep frying French fries and chicken nuggets in fast food places clog the arteries in the worst way. They won't result in heart trouble while your kids are still in grade school, but they will certainly start a bad trend to take into adulthood.

> *"If I'd known I was going to live this long, I'd have taken better care of myself."*
>
> — Eubie Blake (at age 100)

Method Eight:

Cut the Effects of Toxins or Fats by Diluting the Ingredients with Something Healthier

There are certain foods that kids love out of familiarity more than for taste. Canned tuna is one prime example. Most kids like tuna fish sandwiches, even if they won't eat other kinds of fish. But we all know that these days, the mercury level of tuna is unsafe if children eat too much of it. The fish itself, however, is still good for them. I recommend diluting the tuna with a dose of sardines, which are significantly less toxic because they are very low in mercury, and are a great source of essential omega-3 fish oil. This is something children are often missing in their diet. Very few kids will eat sardines straight up. When you mix them with tuna and mayonnaise, though, they happily wolf them down without noticing the difference.

Another example of this method is cutting the amount of heart-clogging butter in a recipe by diluting it with olive oil. This works well for mashed potatoes, grilled cheese, and even buttered toast. You will find that it takes only a small amount of butter to give the dish its buttery taste. Substituting olive oil helps you avoid all that saturated fat. Of course, this method only works with like-substances that match closely in flavor, texture, and color. Other examples are:

- Cutting the fat out of creamy salad dressings by mixing in plain yogurt.
- Using a fruit or vegetable puree in baked goods, again to replace some of the butter.

- Diluting sugar-laden fruit juices with antioxidant-rich green tea or just with water
- Mixing ground turkey or chicken into meatloaf, meatballs and hamburger to cut down on red meat intake
- Using pureed white beans in place of the cream in cream of chicken soup or cream of tomato soup
- Cutting the butter in brownies with purple puree – a combination of blueberries and baby spinach.
- Cutting the butter in cookies with pureed white beans
- Mixing pureed white beans with mayonnaise
- Reducing cheese in lasagna by using pureed tofu (looks just like cheese)

The key with all of these suggestions is to retain enough of the original (less healthy) ingredient so that the flavor of the final product is not different enough to keep the little ones from eating it. As long as the taste, texture, and appearance remain basically the same (or a good decoy is used), you can get away with it. To improve on the method, substitute more of the good stuff each time until you wean them off of the more toxic food.

Health Benefits of Method Eight

Quite simply, this method cuts toxins and generally unhealthy foods from our children's diets. The effects of mercury, especially, add up over time and can contribute to a variety of illnesses. We live in the real world, and cannot avoid many of these foods, which are pushed to your children over every available wavelength of air time. At home, though, you can mitigate the negative impact of them by sneaking them out of the dishes you cook and adding healthier ingredients instead.

Method Nine:

CUT CALORIES AND INCREASE VOLUME WITH LOW-CAL, NUTRITIOUS "FILLERS"

Given that almost one in every three children in this country is overweight, this method takes on extra importance. It involves adding high-volume, nutritious ingredients that have fewer calories per portion in a calorie-dense dish. Think popcorn versus peanuts. Essentially, this "bulks up" the dish, making eaters feel more satisfied, and it is a handy way to avoid overeating. This is similar to "volumetrics," Barbara Roll's system of weight management, which is a fairly new scientific approach to shedding unwanted pounds. It lets people eat as much as they want because basically they won't want too much when the food seems bulky. In this weight-loss system, the meal simply contains more water and fiber. It makes good use of low-calorie, nutritious fillers to satisfy the diner. Examples found in this book will be to add:

• **hidden vegetables to meat sauces.**
• **pureed fruit to homemade ice cream and smoothies.**
• **water or green tea to juice.**
• **low-fat ricotta cheese to ravioli.**
• **pureed vegetables to macaroni and cheese.**
• **pureed vegetables to pasta sauce.**
• **pureed cauliflower to mashed potatoes.**
• **pureed white beans to double stuffed potatoes.**
• **pureed tofu to lasagna.**
• **plain yogurt to ranch dressing.**
• **pureed vegetables to guacamole.**
• **pureed beans and veggies to meat dishes.**
• **vegetables to meatballs.**

A good example of a popular dish that is full of calories and little else is mashed potatoes. By mixing in pureed cauliflower, you increase the amount of "potatoes" in a bowl, but add virtually no more calories. You have tricked the eye and the belly into feeling like you have eaten a lovely bowl of your favorite forbidden food.

Health Benefits of Method Nine

This method chooses ingredients that are high in water, fiber, and nutrients, yet low in fat and sugar. It adds volume to foods that are more calorie-dense and often contain a lot of sugar or fat. Water helps us feel full, while fiber lowers caloric density by providing bulk. Foods that have plenty of both are fruits, vegetables, cooked cereals, and brown rice. We end up consuming far more nutrients while eating the same volume. High-density foods, on the other hand, such as nuts, chips, cheese, and chocolate, are not good candidates. They have high fat and/or calories and sugar and are likely to land at the top of the food pyramid.

Method Ten:
USE SLOWER-BURNING FOODS TO AVOID BLOOD SUGAR "SPIKE AND CRASH"

Foods that are especially high in sugar — even natural sugar and honey — are known to cause a very quick rise in blood-sugar levels. The spike doesn't last very long and is followed by a corresponding fast drop in blood-sugar level. Often it drops even lower than it was before we ate, and it leaves us with a distinct sense of energy depletion.

Children seem especially susceptible to this phenomenon. After they eat the kid-favorite jellybeans (the ultimate sugar spike), particularly when it's on an empty stomach, parents notice them acting as if they've had four cups of coffee. They're bouncing off the walls and then, in a predictable amount of time, they crash — growing sleepy, lethargic, and cranky. The reason is that refined sugars (or carbs) raise blood-glucose levels too quickly, causing a surge of insulin, which soon removes even more sugar than when the person started; the loss of sugar is what makes him feel lethargic. For people who are particularly sensitive, the crash may be accompanied by feelings of shakiness, irritability, fogginess, and intense hunger even though they just ate an hour ago. Any parents with a sensitive child will rush to keep a well meaning adult from giving their child a candy bar as a treat. They know what's coming. Ricocheting around the room like a stray ping-pong ball is bad enough; the bickering with others and the poor concentration only make it worse.

Sugars are not the only culprit. Carbohydrates such as white bread and corn chips, as well as most snack foods and baked goods, produce the same result. Most people don't realize that even vegetables such as white potatoes can have a similar impact on the body. It is called the "glycemic index" (GI)—a measurement of the effect a food has on one's blood sugar level. The higher the rating on the index, the more rapid the increase in blood sugar level. The goal of this method is to slow down the aftereffect. It is also to prevent the longer-term result, which

is that the child ends up craving more of the simple quick-release carbs. Thus begins a vicious cycle of overeating just to keep up one's energy. Almost all packaged snack foods and cereals that are marketed to kids have this effect on them.

Examples of "slow carbs" are high-fiber foods such as whole grain breads and crackers, vegetables, beans, legumes, brown rice, oats, and whole grain pasta. All of these are rated low on the GI for obvious reasons. I recommend that the sneaky chef combine low GI foods *with* spike-and-crash carbs (which unfortunately kids love) to create a lower net effect. A few examples to be found in the recipe section are folding pureed white beans into a stuffed baked potato or adding olive oil and hidden vegetables to sauce on combined whole wheat and white pasta.

As usual, none of the "switches" are obvious. When your kids eat a homemade muffin from this book, all they know is that it's delicious. They crave the high-GI foods, and that is what you appear to be giving them. They get to be satisfied, and you get to relax because there are no ill effects. They stay satisfied longer than if they'd eaten a Krispy Kreme donut, have more sustained energy, feel happier overall, and don't crave as much junk food. Your little muffins won't realize that the muffins they ate had enough fiber from the hidden wheat germ and stone ground flour to stabilize their blood-sugar levels. They have no idea why the Unbelievable Chocolate Chip Cookie was so gratifying to eat. After all, it tasted just like any other chocolate chip cookie, so they couldn't possibly guess that it contained pureed white beans, whole grains, and half the sugar. The only one who knows these little secrets is you (and their healthier bodies).

"Ask your child what

he wants for dinner

only if he's paying."

— *Fran Lebowitz*

Some of the best nutritional boosters you will find in this book are:

- ground slivered almonds in cookies and oatmeal
- pureed white beans and veggies in macaroni and cheese
- wheat germ and pureed beans in cookies
- hidden veggies and beans in pasta with sauce
- pureed vegetables and wheat germ in muffins
- pureed fruit in homemade ice cream and milkshakes
- pureed veggies and oat bran in corn muffins

Health Benefits of Method Ten

The trick here is to combine low-GI foods with high-GI foods. This lowers the GI value of the whole meal and produces a slower rise in glucose.

Typically, the ingredients we are adding are whole foods; that is, they contain the fiber, vitamins, and minerals that have been removed from their processed counterparts.

High-fiber foods not only add nutrients, but they also contribute to the feeling of being full, which prevents children from overeating. Including low-GI foods in recipes keeps the blood sugar levels balanced, reduces subsequent cravings for more sugar and the snacks that contain it, and has a positive influence on moods and concentration, among other things. Fiber also promotes regularity and helps maintain healthy blood cholesterol and triglyceride levels.

Method Eleven:

USE *VISUAL* DECOYS TO MAKE FOOD LOOK APPEALING AND FUN

How many times have your kids rejected a dish based on how it looked and nothing else? How many times have you heard, "Ick! I hate that," and you know perfectly well that they've never tasted it? This method makes us parents into smart marketers, just like the packaged goods companies who use the same tricks to appeal to our kids. Make no mistake about it — you are competing with their multimillion dollar ad campaigns that bombard kids to eat their dolled-up junk food. They know how to make it the right color, shape, or size to seduce your little ones into thinking they have to have it. It's too bad we can't put cartoon characters or superheroes on a bag of fruit or a bundle of vegetables. The kids would be screaming for them. With this method, we still use the junk ingredients, but only a small amount and only as a lure.

All this requires is a little creativity to make the dish kid-friendly. A few of the examples you will find are:

- dusting powdered sugar onto whole-grain Cocoa Chocolate Chip Pancakes
- baking corn bread as mini-muffins and spreading a layer of Incredibly Improved Icing on top, then adding rainbow sprinkles
- cutting french toast into dipping sticks
- serving sorbet in a fun parfait glass with a squirt of whipped cream
- writing your child's initial, with cream, into tomato soup

- serving crunchy chicken tenders on skewers
- making burgers with a mini-bun

Even desserts sometimes need a little help when you're using healthier ingredients. Whole wheat flour blend, for instance, can make cookies look slightly grainier and earthier. A few tricks to make healthy desserts appear even more appealing:

- Make cookies into two-bite minis
- Make super-thick smoothies and call them "Breakfast Ice Cream," and then serve with a squirt of whipped cream
- Garnish a "Quick Fix Chocolate Pudding" with whipped cream

I consistently use a tiny amount of kid-friendly items such as whipped cream (which could make a bucket of rocks look scrumptious), a bright red cherry, colorful sprinkles, chocolate chips, powdered sugar, and cocoa. Often what we are doing is diverting their attention away from the fact that the healthy food doesn't look as white as its counterpart. Whole wheat flour in a pancake can discolor the milkiness of white flour that the kids are used to in boxed pancakes. A dusting of powdered sugar will camoflauge that; so will a drizzle of chocolate syrup or a squirt of whipped cream. A tablespoon of unsweetened cocoa, which is rich in antioxidants, works wonders when you're trying to mask any off-color in muffins, cakes and pancakes. It may bother some moms to give their children Cocoa Chocolate Chip Pancakes for breakfast, but in fact, my recipe has more fruit and fiber in it than a bowl of oat bran with berries.

Health Benefits of Method Eleven

Yes, the decoys themselves aren't particularly healthy. Their purpose is to get the kids to eat the rest of the dish, which *is* healthy. Since we're only adding a small amount of the decoy food, it does very little harm compared to all of the good it's doing. If a mere fifteen calories of whipped cream and sprinkles can trick your children in to eating an entire serving of fiber and vegetables in a whole grain corn muffin laced with wheat germ, cauliflower, and zucchini, isn't it worth it? After all, kids eat plenty of junk food all the time with absolutely no health benefits.

These decoys, simply put, increase your children's intake of everything you want them to eat. They are so appealing that they help the rest of the food evade scrutiny. As such, they are worth their weight in gold.

Method Twelve:

USE KID-FRIENDLY FLAVOR DECOYS TO DISTRACT KIDS FROM WHAT'S UNDERNEATH

Now that we've gotten past the appearance of the food, we have to make sure their tongues are happy too. Whipped cream and sprinkles make only the first bite acceptable; if what comes next is objectionable, they will stop eating right there. Imagine a brownie that looks positively delicious, but leaves the weird aftertaste of broccoli (not a recipe in this book). What kid will want it? One way

to prevent this is by making sure that the superhero ingredients used to fortify the recipes leave no telltale taste of their own— a technique we have already covered. The other way is to use flavors that are bold, and you already know your kids are in love with, to mask any off-tastes.

SOME OF THE FAVORITES ARE:

Cheese on mashed potatoes

Cheddar cheese in whole grain muffins

Chocolate chips in whole grain muffins

Ketchup and brown sugar in baked beans

Chocolate in whole grain baked goods

Ketchup glaze on meatloaf

Ketchup in Bonus Burgers

Ranch dressing in yogurt dips

Do you ever give your children cherry-flavored cough syrup when they're sick? This is the same principle. It simply masks the flavor of something that's good for them. Fortunately, it doesn't take a large amount of their favorite flavors to do the trick. Even if you're adding a tablespoon of sugar, it still represents only a few calories.

This method works because it deceives the tongue and distracts the child from perceiving any new or off-flavors that may otherwise bleed through from the healthy ingredients in the recipe. The flavors listed above are bold enough to overpower most other foods, so the children predominantly pick up on the tastes they are accustomed to. Food companies certainly employ this technique when they load up yogurt with sugar so that people will think it tastes better. In our recipes however, we have far more control over how much of the less healthy substance we are adding. We can, for instance, add a teaspoon of sugar to plain yogurt, not four tablespoons.

Health Benefits of Method Twelve

The health benefits of this method are essentially the same as the previous one. By using a minimal amount of their favorite flavoring, we trick our kids into eating healthy ingredients. Though packaged goods may use the same idea, we parents, can make sure our kids are consuming far fewer sweeteners, saturated fats, and so on. In addition— and this is of particular importance—we are in the position to add far more nutrition to the main dish than General Mills does. Our muffins, with their seemingly sinful decoy ingredients, still have more to recommend them than Hostess Twinkies.

Method Thirteen:
USE KID-FRIENDLY TEXTURE DECOYS

In this last method, we need to be concerned with the texture of foods, especially with children, whose palates are extremely astute. Something may look and taste great, but if it is lumpy or gritty or leafy, and the kids aren't expecting that at all, they won't go anywhere near it. Don't panic. There are a few simple, yet highly effective ways to change the texture of a recipe so that it is kid-friendly.

We have mentioned some of these ingredients before. They tend to pull double duty. Sprinkles, for example. Simply by mixing in a few sprinkles, the tongue is redirected toward them and away from the slight difference in texture. Here are a few more examples that you'll find in this book that make use of this method:

- When you add pureed avocado to chocolate pudding, cover with sprinkles or chocolate chips.
- When you add spinach and blueberries to brownies, top them with sprinkles while the chocolate is still hot.
- When you add wheat germ to peanut butter, mix in chocolate chips.
- When you add cauliflower to macaroni and cheese, add extra cheese to make the dish creamier.
- When you add wheat germ to French toast, add crushed cereal topping to make the covering crunchier.
- When you use the Flour Blend in this book for cookies, add chocolate chips to mask the texture change.
- When you add oat bran to your kids' oatmeal, add either raisins or chocolate chips.

Health Benefits of Method Thirteen

Many, many healthy ingredients are going to add a texture that turns kids off. For whatever reason, vegetables and whole grains lack a certain appeal. Yet we want our kids to eat them. The crunchiness of the decoys is a great distraction for the mouth. Kids just don't pay attention to what is underneath the crunch, so you know they're consuming a full ration of the right kinds of food in spite of their off-putting texture. This method significantly increases the odds that when you place your carefully prepared dish on the table, they will chow it down. The number of calories added by the decoys is minimal, yet they act as a great lure. This gives you the freedom to add even more healthy ingredients to your recipes.

Here's a handy key to all of the icons, which will accompany the recipes in chapter 7.

 Method One: Puree

 Method Two: Combine Refined and Unrefined

 Method Three: Use Foods That Hide Well

 Method Four: Substitute Nutritious Liquid for Water When Boiling Foods

 Method Five: Combine Foods that are a Specific Nutritional Complement for Each Other

 Method Six: Identify Foods Kids are Likely to Enjoy Straight-Up

 Method Seven: Alter the Cooking Method to Avoid Frying

 Method Eight: Cut the Effects of Toxins or Fats by Diluting the Ingredients with Something Healthier

 Method Nine: Cut Calories and Increase Volume with Low-Cal, Nutritious "Fillers"

Method Ten: Use Slower-Burning Foods to Avoid Blood Sugar "Spike and Crash"

 Method Eleven: Use Visual Decoys to Make Food Look Appealing and Fun

Method Twelve: Use Kid-Friendly Flavor Decoys to Distract Kids From What's Underneath

 Method Thirteen: Use Kid-Friendly Texture Decoys

CHAPTER SIX

Make-Ahead Recipes

Now that we understand what's inside the sneaky chef's bag of tricks, let's put these clever methods into action.

I didn't really have to do an official sampling of kids' restaurant menus across the nation to figure out the top foods they want to eat. After all, I have witnessed firsthand the eating habits of my children and their friends. However, I did conduct my own informal study, just to confirm the national study and bolster my findings. According to the Center for Science in the Public Interest, which investigates these issues in a serious way, fried chicken (fingers or nuggets) is on every one of twenty kids' menus reviewed nationwide, and more than 85 percent of the menus offer burgers. French fries, hash browns, pizza, macaroni and cheese, and spaghetti and meatballs also top the lists. Since we know that these are meals kids like to eat, I have provided a healthy version of them all in this book.

I have spent years conducting kitchen research and testing using nice, unsuspecting children as my little lab rats to bring you their favorite foods. The only difference is that my recipes are cleverly injected with the world's healthiest ingredients to make them into superfoods. A few of the items, such as canned SpaghettiOs, may make some parents shudder. These are the ones you fight against every day because they seem to represent the least healthy food you could imagine feeding your kids.

But guess what: This is an enemy you have to collaborate with, because if you try to fight it you can't win. For reasons known only to space aliens, kids love these products. Everything in the known universe is stacked up against us in our battle against them— our children's friends, advertising, packaging, television, you name it— all collaborators with the enemy. And then there's us, all by ourselves, fighting a valiant battle. However, given that they're going to eat these foods anyway, why not use them to your advantage and maximize the nutritional benefits by adding hidden ingredients? It's like turning the enemy into a friend, into a delivery system for the nutrients you can't get into them any other way. Now some of these combinations will seem odd to you. Spinach in brownies? Avocado in smoothies? Don't be alarmed. Rest assured that every recipe has been adult-, kid-, and-kitchen tested and they all work beautifully and flawlessly. With very few exceptions (e.g., the kid who will only eat one thing—white

bread with butter—until he's thirteen), kids devour them without notice or complaint. The taste is as close to "normal" as it can get, given the quality of what's in these recipes.

Time, of course, is every modern parent's main concern. Even if you aren't working full time, you are trying to keep a lot of balls in the air at once. The question all of you will be asking is, "How much longer will it take me to turn ordinary recipes into super-recipes?" The Make-Ahead purees and blends contain most of the recognized superfoods, and these are used over and over in this book. All you have to do is frontload your week by putting a little time into preparing the Make-Aheads, and you're all set to transform ordinary recipes into health food. And even if you haven't prepared the Make-Aheads, they only take about ten minutes. (It's the steaming part that is time consuming.) Mostly, all you are doing is dumping ingredients into the food processor and pressing the "on" button. So, what do we have? One master shopping list per week and one half-hour session to prepare all of your Make-Aheads (which take less than ten minutes prep time apiece).

Even if you opt for the scratch recipes, you'll spend less than thirty minutes for each one. "Quick Fixes"—those recipes that begin with pre-packaged foods— are for those of us who can't always make recipes from the ground up with fresh ingredients, but want to upgrade what our kids eat anyway. All changes to the Quick Fixes add fewer than five minutes time to the package directions and most incorporate the Make-Ahead purees and blends.

At the top of each recipe, I have simplified the nutritional information so that moms can keep track of how much more nutrition their kids are taking in every week. In addition to a list of key nutrients in each recipe, I have also listed nutrition highlights so that it's easy to decipher the pertinent information. These nutrition highlights are somewhat parallel to the new USDA food guidelines. They indicate the key benefits of the recipe, such as whole grains, fruit, vegetables, calcium, beans, nuts, and even good omega-3 oils.

For all of the purees, the instructions call for a food processor. I highly recommend a three-cup mini processor, (my personal favorite—and top rated—is KitchenAid's 3-cup Chef's Chopper® series, available on my website). There are five good reasons for using a mini processor. One, they're inexpensive. Two, they're easy to leave on the countertop all of the time because they don't take up much space. (I don't know about you, but if I have to find an appliance in the cupboard, I don't use it.) Three, they work well with the relatively small amounts of ingredients in these recipes. Four, they're easier to operate than the large processors. And five, there are fewer parts to wash, so clean-up is quicker. However, you don't need this piece of equipment to use this book. You can use either the larger food processor (although you might want to double the recipes) or a blender. The secret with the blender is to either use a little more liquid, which you put in first, or stop frequently and push the ingredients to the bottom.

Make-Ahead Recipe #1: Purple Puree

3 cups raw baby spinach leaves (or 2 cups frozen chopped spinach, or frozen chopped collard greens)

1½ cups fresh or frozen blueberries (no syrup or sugar added)

1 teaspoon lemon juice

3–4 tablespoons water

If using raw spinach, thoroughly wash it, even if the package says "prewashed." Bring spinach or collards and water to boil in a medium pot. Turn heat to low and allow to simmer for 10 minutes. If using frozen blueberries, quickly rinse them under cold water to thaw a little, and then drain.

Fill the bowl of your food processor with the blueberries and cooked spinach, (or collards) along with the lemon juice and 2 tablespoons of water, and puree on high until as smooth as possible. Stop occasionally to push top contents to bottom. If necessary, add the rest of the water to make a fairly smooth puree.

This amount of spinach and blueberries makes only about 1 cup of puree. Double the recipe if you want to store another cup of the puree. It will store in the refrigerator up to 2 days, or you can freeze ¼ cup portions in sealed plastic bags or small plastic containers.

Purple Puree is used in the following recipes:

Cocoa Chocolate Chip Pancakes

Health-by-Chocolate Cookies

Brainy Brownies

Quick-Fix for Store-Bought Brownie Mix

Total Tacos

Bonus Burgers

Choc-ful Donuts / Choc-ful Cupcakes

NUTRITIONAL INFORMATION FOR PURPLE PUREE:

Blueberries—Researchers at the USDA have ranked blueberries #1 in antioxidant power in comparison to forty other fresh fruits and vegetables. They contain powerful flavonoids, a group of substances that possess antioxidant properties. As one of the most nutrient-dense fruits, blueberries are bursting with vitamins A and C, zinc, potassium, iron, calcium, and magnesium, and they're also high in fiber. Evidence is pouring in about their power to boost immunity to everyday illnesses, to prevent disease in the future, and to protect the heart even more than red wine does. Cranberries are famous for offering protection against urinary tract infections. Now blueberries are being credited with the same advantage. They are also especially high in lutein, which keeps eyes healthy. Researchers have even found that diets rich in blueberries can significantly improve memory function, learning capacity and motor skills, making kids not only healthier but also smarter.

Spinach—Spinach is a nutrient powerhouse. It contains twice as much iron as most other greens and is an excellent source of calcium, folic acid, and vitamins A and C. Its beta carotene content (Surprise! It's not even orange) offers great protection against asthma, all kinds of cancer, and heart disease. It also protects the eyes, growing bones, and brains.

Make-Ahead Recipe #2: Orange Puree

1 medium sweet potato
  or yam, peeled and
  rough chopped
3 medium to large carrots,
  peeled and sliced into
  thick chunks
3–4 tablespoons water

In a medium pot, cover carrots and sweet potatoes with cold water and boil for about 20 minutes until yams, and especially carrots, are very tender. If the carrots aren't thoroughly cooked, they'll leave telltale little nuggets of vegetables, which will reveal their presence (a gigantic no-no for the sneaky chef).

Drain the yams and carrots and put them in the food processor with two tablespoons of water. Puree on high until smooth; no chunks should remain. Stop occasionally to push the contents from the top to the bottom. If necessary, add the rest of the water to make a smooth puree, but the less water the better.

This makes about 2 cups of puree. Double the recipe if you want to store another cup of puree. Store in refrigerator up to three days, or freeze ¼ cup portions in sealed plastic bags or small plastic containers.

Orange Puree is used in the following recipes:

Fortified French Toast

Masterful Mac 'n' Cheese

Quick Fixes for Boxed Macaroni
  and Cheese

Guerrilla Grilled Cheese

Packed Pizza Bagels

Quick Fixes for SpaghettiOs

"Saucy" Meat Sauce

Crunchy Chicken Tenders

Maxed Out Meatloaf

Easy Homemade Pasta Sauce

Quick Fixes for Store-Bought Tomato Sauce

Franks 'n' Beans

Pigs in Healthy Blankets

Bravo Nacho Cheese Dip

Power Pizza

Creative Cream of Tomato Soup

Tricky Taco Soup

Covert Quesadillas

Sneaky Baked Ziti

Thumbprint Peanut Butter Cookies

Peanut Butter and Jelly Muffins

Grilled Cheese Muffins

NUTRITIONAL INFORMATION FOR ORANGE PUREE:

Carrots are anything but ordinary. With its vibrant orange color, it is more than "good for your eyes." Known as the "king of vegetables," carrots are the richest source of carotenes and antioxidants among them all. Some studies have shown that as little as one carrot per day could possibly cut the risk of lung cancer in half. These orange beauties boost immunity, they're full of fiber—more than two grams in one carrot, they strengthen the heart, and they protect against most cancers. The nutrients are even better absorbed when carrots are cooked, as they are in this puree. Pureed carrots are also a helpful remedy to cut diarrhea short and speed the recovery time from illnesses.

Sweet Potatoes and Yams are packed with antioxidant vitamins C and E, carotenes, calcium, potassium, and iron. Rich in complex carbohydrates and fiber, sweet potatoes are known as the "anti-diabetic" food because they stabilize blood sugar levels, preventing "crash and burn." They're also a good source of B vitamins and folate, which strengthen and protect the heart and have been proven to boost brain power. Sweet potatoes have good reason to be called a comfort food. Besides being filling, satisfying, and incredibly nutritious, they're known to boost the mood-elevating levels of serotonin, which calms children and even gets them to sleep better. They also add a subtle sweetness to sneaky recipes and work doubly hard to cut acidity when combined with tomato sauce, which can cause indigestion.

Make-Ahead Recipe #3: Green Puree

2 cups raw baby spinach leaves (or 1 cup frozen chopped spinach, or frozen chopped collard greens)

2 cups broccoli florets, fresh or frozen

1 cup sweet green peas, frozen

1 teaspoon fresh lemon juice

3–4 tablespoons water

If using raw spinach, thoroughly wash it, even if the package says "prewashed." Using a vegetable steamer, steam broccoli and spinach (or collards) in 2 inches of water in a tightly covered pot for about 10 minutes. Add the frozen peas for the last minute of steaming. Alternatively, place broccoli, spinach (or collards) in a microwave-safe bowl, cover with water, and microwave on high for 8 to 10 minutes until very tender, adding the frozen peas for the last minute of cooking.

Once cooked, drain the vegetables and place them in the bowl of your food processor along with 2 tablespoons of water and lemon juice. Puree on high until as smooth as possible. Stop occasionally and push contents from the top to the bottom. If necessary, add the rest of the water to make a smoother puree.

Makes about 2 cups of puree. Double this recipe if you want to store an extra cup. Store in refrigerator up to 3 days, or freeze ¼ cup portions in sealed plastic bags or small plastic containers.

Green Puree is used in the following recipes:

Maxed Out Meatloaf

Magic Meatballs

No Harm Chicken Parm

No Doc Guac

Undercover Crispy Ravioli

NUTRITIONAL INFORMATION FOR GREEN PUREE:

Spinach See page 97

Broccoli is one of the most nutrient-dense, healthy foods on the planet, and with the exception of kids (and famously George H. W. Bush), it happens to be a favorite of most other Americans. Broccoli is high in protein and fiber. In just one half cup, you get 2 grams of fiber and 100 percent of the recommended daily value of vitamin C. This antioxidant boosts immunity against everyday colds, the flu, heart disease, and all cancers. As one of the best vegetable sources of calcium, it also strengthens growing bones and teeth.

Green Peas A good source of fiber, vitamin C and potassium, these little wonders help boost immunity and have great cold-fighting potential. They also protect against heart disease and all types of cancer. They're high in the little known vitamin K, which strengthens bones, and they're high in iron, which provides greater energy levels and improved learning. Incredibly, one cup of green peas actually has more protein than a large egg.

Make-Ahead Recipe #4: White Puree

2 cups cauliflower, cut
  into florets

2 small to medium
  zucchini, peeled and
  roughly chopped

1 teaspoon fresh lemon
  juice

3–4 tablespoons water,
  if necessary

Steam cauliflower in a vegetable steamer over 2 inches of water, using a tightly-covered pot, for about 10 to 12 minutes until very tender. Alternatively, place cauliflower in a microwave-safe bowl, cover with water, and microwave on high for 8 to 10 minutes until very tender.

While waiting for the cauliflower to finish steaming, start to pulse the *raw* peeled zucchini with the lemon juice only (no water at this point). Drain the cooked cauliflower. Working in batches if necessary, add it to the pulsed zucchini in the bowl of the food processor with two tablespoons of water. Puree on high until smooth. Stop occasionally and push contents from the top to the bottom. If necessary, add the rest of the water to make a smooth puree.

Makes about 2 cups of puree. Double recipe if you want to store even more, which can be done in the refrigerator for up to 3 days, or freeze ¼ cup portions in sealed plastic bags or the small plastic containers.

White Puree is used in the following recipes:

Masterful Mac 'n' Cheese

Quick Fixes for Boxed Macaroni
  and Cheese

Quick Fixes for SpaghettiOs

Triple Stuffed Potatoes

Gotta Lotta Lasagna

NUTRITIONAL INFORMATION FOR WHITE PUREE:

Zucchini is low in calories but high in fiber, manganese, vitamin C, and potassium, offering protection against asthma, many cancers, high blood pressure and heart disease. Other benefits include muscle strengthening, enhanced energy, clearer thinking, and a happier disposition. Their delicate flavor and creamy white flesh make them an ideal choice for sneaky chefs.

Cauliflower is packed with vitamin C, folate and fiber. It enhances immunity and fights disease almost as well as its cousin, broccoli. A large preliminary study has shown that young children who have asthma experience significantly less wheezing if they eat a diet high in foods rich in vitamin C. Vitamin C is a powerful antioxidant that may protect against bruising and is needed to maintain healthy bones and skin. It strengthens the immune system, helping to prevent and fight colds, flu, and other illnesses.

Make-Ahead Recipe #5: Green Juice

3 cups raw baby spinach leaves (or 2 cups frozen chopped spinach, or frozen chopped collard greens)

1 cup water

If using raw spinach, thoroughly wash it, even if the package says "prewashed." Bring spinach or collards and water to boil in a medium pot. Turn heat to low and allow to simmer for 10 minutes. Pour into a fine mesh strainer over a container or bowl, pressing the green "pulp" with the back of a spoon until all the liquid is released.

Store in refrigerator for up to 3 days, or freeze ¼ cup portions in sealed plastic bags or small plastic containers. This makes about 1 cup of Green juice. Double the recipe if you want to store another cup of juice.

Green Juice is used in the following recipes:

Quick Fixes for Store-Bought
 Chocolate Pudding
Earth Day Milk Shake

Chocolate Shake
Popeye's Eggs
Green Icing

NUTRITIONAL INFORMATION FOR GREEN JUICE:

Green Juice is an extremely nutrient-dense food. One tablespoon of it is comparable to eating about ¼ cup of spinach leaves. It has been boiled for safety, and it possesses the motherlode of nutrients like iron, calcium, and enzymes for digestion, as well as chlorophyll and carotenes for disease-fighting power.

Make-Ahead Recipe #6: Blueberry Juice

2½ cups fresh or frozen blueberries (no syrup or sugar added)

2 cups water

1 tablespoon sugar

Bring berries, water and sugar to boil in a medium pot. Turn heat to low and allow to simmer for 10 minutes. Occasionally mash the blueberries with the back of a spoon to release their juices. Pour into a fine mesh strainer over a container or bowl, pressing the blueberry "pulp" with the back of a spoon until all the liquid is released.

Store in refrigerator up to 3 days, or freeze ¼ cup portions in sealed plastic bags or small plastic containers. Makes 2 cups of Blueberry Juice. Double this recipe if you want to store more juice. This recipe also yields about ¾ cup pulp leftover in the strainer. Save this pulp to add to Purple Puree, or smoothies.

Blueberry Juice is used in the following recipes:

Quick Fixes for Jell-O

Jiggly Gelatin Blocks

Royal Ice Pops

Blue Ribbon Shake

Lavender Icing

Frozen Applesauce

Blueberry Milk

Quick Fixes for Store-Bought Lemonade

Quick Fixes for Applesauce

Homemade Berry Syrup

Say **Yes** to Sorbet

Quick Fixes for Sparkling Water

Quick Fixes for Oatmeal

NUTRITIONAL INFORMATION FOR BLUEBERRY JUICE:

Blueberry Juice—Blueberries' purple color indicates they are rich in anthocyanins and ellagic acid —powerful cancer fighters and brain boosters.

Blueberry Juice also offers anti-bacterial activity that can combat intestinal infections due to E.Coli, and are an effective treatment for cystitis.

Make-Ahead Recipe #7: Cherry Juice

2½ cups fresh or frozen
pitted cherries (no syrup
or sugar added)
2 cups water
1 tablespoon sugar

Bring cherries, water, and sugar to boil in a medium pot. Turn heat to low and allow to simmer for 10 minutes. Occasionally mash the cherries with the back of a spoon (or a potato masher) to release their juices. Pour into a fine mesh strainer over a container or bowl, pressing the cherry "pulp" with the back of a spoon until all the liquid is released.

Store in refrigerator up to 3 days, or freeze ¼ cup portions in sealed plastic bags or small plastic containers. Makes 2 cups of Cherry Juice. Double this recipe if you want to store more juice. This recipe also yields about ¾ cup pulp leftover in the strainer. Save this pulp to add to smoothies.

Cherry Juice is used in the following recipes:

Frozen Applesauce

Chocolate Milk

Cheery Hot Cocoa

Quick Fixes for Store-Bought Lemonade

Quick Fixes for Jell-O®

Royal Ice Pops

Say **Yes** to Sorbet

Quick Fixes for Sparkling Water

Quick Fixes for Oatmeal

NUTRITIONAL INFORMATION FOR CHERRY JUICE:

Cherry Juice is referred to by some nutritionists as the "healing fruit"; cherries are rich in vitamins A, C, potassium, fiber and antioxidants. Like blueberries, cherries are a potent source of ellagic acid — a flavonoid that has been found to be one of the most potent anti-cancer agents. Studies have shown that cherries, especially the tart ones, can help educe inflammation in the body and therefore can help eliminate migraine headaches—similar to aspirin or ibuprofen. They are also rich in the naturally-occurring hormone melatonin which has been found to slow aging and enhance sleep. And to top it off, researchers report that cherries can slow the spoilage of ground beef and reduce the formation of potentially harmful compounds in meat during cooking.

Try to use **organic** frozen or fresh cherries and strawberries, since both of these fruits are on the "dirty dozen" list—the produce most contaminated with pesticide residues.

Make-Ahead Recipe #8: Strawberry Juice

2½ cups fresh or frozen
    strawberries (no syrup
    or sugar added)

2 cups water

1 tablespoon sugar

Bring berries, water and sugar to boil in a medium pot. Turn heat to low and allow to simmer for 10 minutes. Occasionally mash the strawberries with the back of a spoon to release their juices. Pour into a fine mesh strainer over a container or bowl, pressing the strawberry "pulp" with the back of a spoon until all the liquid is released.

Store in refrigerator up to 3 days, or freeze ¼ cup portions in sealed plastic bags or small plastic containers. Makes 2 cups of Strawberry Juice. Double this recipe if you want to store more juice. This recipe also yields about ¾ cup pulp leftover in the strainer. Save this pulp to add to smoothies.

Strawberry Juice is used in the following recipes:

Frozen Applesauce

Strawberry Milk

Quick Fixes for Store-Bought Lemonade

Quick Fixes for Jell-O®

Royal Ice Pops

Homemade Berry Syrup

Say **Yes** to Sorbet

Quick Fixes for Sparkling Water

Quick Fixes for Oatmeal

NUTRITIONAL INFORMATION FOR STRAWBERRY JUICE:

Strawberry Juice Strawberries' dark red color means great health benefits from the potent antioxidants and rich supply of vitamins. Just eight strawberries provide 140 percent of the recommended daily intake of vitamin C for children, and they are also a good source of folic acid, fiber, potassium, and disease-fighting phytochemicals. Strawberry Juice offers a concentrated dose of these immune-boosting nutrients.

Make-Ahead Recipe #9: White Bean Puree

1 15-ounce can white beans
(great northern, navy,
butter or cannellini)
(If you are starting
with dry beans, soak
overnight and cook as
directed)

2 to 3 tablespoons water

Rinse and drain the beans and put in the bowl of your food processor. Pulsing in on/off turns, puree the drained beans with two tablespoon of water in processor until smooth, stopping occasionally to scrape down sides of bowl. The goal is a smooth, but *not wet*, puree. (You are aiming for the consistency of peanut butter.) If necessary, thin with a little more water until there are no flecks of whole beans visible.

Store in the refrigerator up to 3 days, or freeze ¼ cup portions in sealed plastic bags or small plastic containers. Makes about 1 cup of puree. Double this recipe if you want to store another cup of puree.

White Bean Puree is used in the following recipes:

Quick Fixes for Boxed Macaroni and Cheese

Quick Fixes for Tuna Fish Sandwiches

IQ Tuna Patties

Packed Pizza Bagels

Quick Fixes for SpaghettiOs

"Saucy" Meat Sauce

Triple Stuffed Potatoes

Unbelievable Chocolate Chip Cookies

Quick Fixes for Store-Bought Tomato Sauce

Pigs in Healthy Blankets

Power Pizza

Creamy Chicken Noodle Soup

Tricky Taco Soup

Covert Quesadillas

Sneaky Baked Ziti

Mystery Mashed Potatoes

No Sin Potato Skins

Leftover Potato Cakes

NUTRITIONAL INFORMATION FOR WHITE BEAN PUREE:

Beans White beans such as navy, butter or cannellini, are inexpensive and incredibly satisfying and nutritious. They've been found to lower cholesterol and blood pressure, and to prevent constipation. When added to high-carb/high-sugar foods, beans help stabilize blood-sugar levels, providing steady, slow-burning energy so the kids will feel satisfied longer and have less "brain fog." All beans are excellent sources of folate and tryptophan, as well as magnesium and iron, providing energy and power to boost the brain and protect against heart disease and cancer. White beans can increase energy by helping to replenish iron stores. This is especially important for children, who are at risk for iron deficiency.

Combined with grains or rice, beans form a whole protein comparable to meat and dairy. Their creamy white color and very mild flavor make them excellent sneaky ingredients in many recipes.

Make-Ahead Recipe #10: Chickpea Puree

1 15-ounce can chickpeas (a.k.a. garbanzo beans) (If you prefer to use whole beans, soak overnight and cook as directed)

2 to 3 tablespoons water

Rinse and drain chickpeas and put in the bowl of your food processor. Using on/off turns, puree drained chickpeas with just two tablespoons of water until smooth, stopping occasionally to scrape down sides of bowl. The goal is a smooth, but *not wet*, puree. If necessary, thin with a little more water, until no more flecks of chickpeas are visible.

Store in refrigerator up to 3 days, or freeze ¼ cup portions in sealed plastic bags or small plastic containers. Makes about 1 cup of puree. Double this recipe if you want to store another cup of puree.

Chickpea Puree is used in the following recipes:

Bonus Burgers

Cheesy Animal Crackers

NUTRITIONAL INFORMATION FOR CHICKPEA PUREE:

Chickpeas—Inexpensive and incredibly satisfying and nutritious, chickpeas have been found to lower cholesterol and blood pressure and prevent constipation. Like white beans, when they're added to high-carb/high-sugar foods, they stabilize blood sugar levels, providing steady, slow-burning energy so that the kids will feel satisfied longer and feel less "dazed and confused" after the meal.

All beans are an excellent source of folate and tryptophan, magnesium and iron, providing a great source of energy, brain-boosting power, and protection against heart disease and cancer. Chickpeas can especially increase energy by helping to replenish iron stores. This is particularly important for children who are more at risk for iron deficiency.

Make-Ahead Recipe #11: Frozen Bananas

Bananas, ripe

Use bananas that are overripe and speckled with brown spots. (They have more natural sugars in them at this stage.) Peel and break each one into 3 or 4 pieces. Freeze in sealed plastic bags to use in shakes and other recipes.

Frozen Bananas are used in the following recipes:

Banana Breakfast Ice Cream

Chocolate Banana Breakfast Ice Cream

NUTRITIONAL INFORMATION FOR FROZEN BANANAS:

Bananas—A great staple to have on hand, frozen bananas are the nutrient-dense, sweet, non-fat, thickening base for quick homemade ice cream, smoothies, and milk shakes. Most athletes appreciate the energy delivered by bananas' high levels of potassium, as well as their complex carbohydrates for slow-burning energy. Since they neutralize stomach acid, they are easily digestible, even when children are feeling a little queasy. Bananas are so mild that they're often given to babies as their first solid food.

"Bananas are binding," we've been told, meaning they help alleviate the discomfort of loose stools. Yet they also contain as much fiber as a slice of whole grain bread and the pectin of an apple, both of which maintain good intestinal health. In addition, bananas contain tryptophan, a very calming nutrient. They can replace the electrolytes lost from bouts with diarrhea and even help build better bones by improving the body's ability to absorb calcium. As if that weren't enough, bananas nourish the "good" bacteria in the colon (probiotics), the stuff that promotes wholesome digestion and strengthens the immune system.

Make-Ahead Recipe #12: Better Breading

----

1 cup bread crumbs,
    preferably whole wheat

1 cup almonds, slivered
    and blanched (optional;
    omit if allergic)

1 cup wheat germ,
    unsweetened

1 teaspoon salt

With this recipe, you are aiming at the consistency of cornmeal. Pulse almonds in food processor. Don't let the food processor run continually; if you don't pulse it, you will end up with nut butter. Pour the meal into a bowl, and then combine into it the ground bread crumbs, wheat germ, and salt.

Keep refrigerated in a sealed, labeled plastic bag for up to 2 weeks.

Sneaky Tip:

Whole wheat bread crumbs can be found in natural and organic food stores, but you can easily make your own by pulsing whole grain bread in a food processor to achieve fine crumbs. It's that simple. Three slices of bread yield about one cup of fresh crumbs. They keep for weeks in a sealed bag in the freezer.

Better Breading is used in the following recipes:

Crunchy Chicken Tenders

No Harm Chicken Parm

Hi-Fi Fish Sticks

Crunchy Elbows

NUTRITIONAL INFORMATION FOR BETTER BREADING:

Wheat Germ is a real powerhouse of nutrients, offering an excellent source of iron, protein, B vitamins, folic acid, and vitamin E. It is one of the best food sources of zinc, magnesium, manganese, and chromium. The B vitamins nourish the whole nervous system and may help prevent fatigue and migraine headaches.

Almonds are packed with nutrition and the "good" heart-healthy oils like those from olives. Just a quarter-cup of almonds boasts more protein than an egg. In addition, they're rich in magnesium, potassium, calcium, iron, zinc, and vitamin E. They have been found to lower bad cholesterol while improving the good kind, and they provide soluble fiber and antioxidants to strengthen the heart and fight disease.

New research also suggests that the fiber in almonds may actually help combat obesity and diabetes—even though they are relatively high in fat themselves—by blocking the body's absorption of both fat and carbohydrates, keeping weight down and blood sugar stabilized. Almonds are also very satisfying. Anything enhanced by their flavor and texture will provide a sustained source of energy.

Make-Ahead Recipe #13: Flour Blend

1 cup all-purpose,
   unbleached white flour

1 cup whole wheat flour

1 cup wheat germ,
   unsweetened

Combine the flours and wheat germ in a bowl. This blend can be stored in a sealed, labeled plastic bag for months.

Sneaky Tip:

A quick replacement for my Flour Blend is Eagle Mills All-Purpose Flour made with Ultragrain©. It's already blended for you! Cup for cup, you'll get more whole grain nutrition than in white flour—with the great taste, color and texture you expect.

Flour Blend is used in the following recipes:

Unbelievable Chocolate Chip Cookies

Health-by-Chocolate Cookies

Brainy Brownies

Choc-ful Donuts / Choc-ful Cupcakes

Breakfast Cookies and Milk

Thumbprint Peanut Butter Cookies

Cheesy Animal Crackers

Peanut Butter and Jelly Muffins

Grilled Cheese Muffins

Complete Corn Muffins

NUTRITIONAL INFORMATION FOR FLOUR BLEND:

Wheat Germ —see page 119

Whole Wheat Flour features many important nutrients that ultimately get stripped away when wheat is further processed into white flour. Whole wheat is an excellent source of manganese, magnesium and tryptophan. It is rich in fiber, which helps regulate digestion, prevents constipation, and stabilizes blood sugar levels, making us feel satisfied longer. It also protects against insulin resistance that can be a precursor to diabetes.

Whole grains can help fight obesity as well. A Harvard Medical School study published in the November 2003 issue of the **American Journal of Clinical Nutrition** showed that women who consumed more fiber-rich whole grains weigh less than those who eat more refined wheat products, and those consuming the most dietary fiber from whole grains were 49 percent less likely to gain weight compared to those eating foods made from refined grains.

INSTANT SUPERMARKET PUREES:

Note: Some Make-Aheads are actually prepared for you by the food industry, even though they aren't aware that they're helping you become a sneaky chef. If you find yourself short of time, or if you're in the midst of a recipe and you don't have a Make-Ahead on hand, some purees used in this book (although not all) can be purchased from the food manufacturers. Baby foods are an especially good source because the fruits and vegetables are already pureed.

Sneaky Tip:

Other useful instant supermaket purees are tomato paste, applesauce, unsweetened fruit spread, and fresh, ripe avocados (mashed).

In the case of baby foods-as-puree, I have found that the Beech-Nut brand works best as an instant substitute. I'm all about feeding my family the best quality food I can find, and I discovered that Beech-Nut is very innovative in their use of natural ingredients, has extremely high quality standards even though their products are not officially "organic." Unlike other large company brands— even organic lines—their purees contain no sugar, modified food starch, thickeners or other additives. They have also taken a leadership role in keeping pesticide residue to an absolute minimum, making their products comparable to those containing organically-grown fruits and vegetables. What's more, you don't have to go to a specialty food store to find Beech-Nut—it's widely distributed in the US, and can be found in most supermarkets across the country.

MAKE AHEAD	INGREDIENTS	INSTANT SUBSTITUTE
White Puree	cauliflower/ zucchini	baby food zucchini
Orange Puree	sweet potatoes/carrots	baby food sweet potatoes and carrots
Green Puree	broccoli	baby food peas, and garden vegetables
Purple Puree	blueberries/spinach	baby food apples and blueberries
White Bean Puree	white beans	vegetarian refried pinto beans (these are darker in color, and not as bland as white beans) – they would work only with darker colored meat and tomato sauce)
Blueberry Juice	blueberries	bottled blueberry or pomegranate juice
Strawberry Juice	strawberries	bottled strawberry or pomegranate juice
Cherry Juice	cherries	bottled apple/cherry juice
Green Juice	spinach	pick up at health food store or at a juice bar

CHAPTER SEVEN

Recipes

As you dive into the following recipes, you will find that the Make-Aheads from chapter 6 are your best friends. These recipes are designed to be super fast and easy, and the Make-Aheads help accomplish this. Once you have these purees and blends in your refrigerator or freezer, simply grab a spoonful and mix it into the recipes as called for.

JUST A FEW NOTES BEFORE WE BEGIN:

1. Regarding the "Optional Extra Boost" noted at the bottom of most recipes: This is an undisguised, visible ingredient that will add quite a bit of nutrition, but it is decidedly not meant to be hidden . . . your kids will spot it. Before adding the ingredient, be sure they like this food or you risk ruining the entire recipe.

2. At the top of each recipe, I've indicated which sneaky methods are used from my bag of tricks in Chapter 5. Each method is identified by an icon.

3. For each recipe, the sneaky ingredients are highlighted in grey type.

4. All of the purees and juices can be frozen for future use for up to three months.

5. You can store ¼ to ½ cup portions of the purees, which is the amount that most of

my recipes call for, in sealed plastic bags or small plastic containers and freeze them. This practice makes it enormously easy to use this book.

6. In general, I suggest using a small amount of the puree for the first few times you serve a recipe. Gradually increase the amount of the booster over time, adding a much as you can get away with. (If you go too far, just scale back and try again.) Children are then acclimated to any subtle changes that the Make-Aheads might add.

7. Many recipes in this book call for "salt." I have not specified what type of salt in each recipe, but would highly suggest considering using a natural, crystal salt that contains a complete spectrum of minerals that your body is able to utilize. Common table salt has been highly processed (like white bread) and stripped of its natural mineral elements. One of the easiest and most positive impacts you can make on your family's health is to invest in a really good salt, like the Original Himalayan Crystal Salt. Research reveals it is even healthier than the sea salt sold in natural food stores.

So whip the top off your mini food processor and line up the überfoods. You are now armed and ready to make *The Sneaky Chef* a part of your family's daily life. One day they'll thank you. In the meantime, try to keep a straight face at the dinner table.

BREAKFAST RECIPES

Chocolate Chip Pancakes

Nutrition Highlights: Whole grains, fruit, calcium, nuts, and protein · Rich in vitamins C and E, fiber, calcium, and protein

Kids may love to eat ordinary pancakes such as Aunt Jemima, but the ingredients consist of bleached white flour, eggs, oil, and water. Since this healthy recipe calls for whole wheat flour and wheat germ, the pancakes have a slightly denser quality. Hence, we put in chocolate chips as a texture and flavor decoy.

One of the conveniences of this recipe is that you can actually make the batter the night before for freshly made pancakes every day of the week, or you can place the cooked pancakes in a plastic bag and freeze them for months, then simply toast them in the morning. They also hold up well as a "grab and go" hand-held breakfast in the car on the way to school.

MAKES ABOUT 18 PANCAKES

¾ cups Flour Blend (see Make-Ahead Recipe #13)

1 teaspoon baking powder

½ teaspoon salt

¼ cup blanched, slivered almonds, finely ground in a food processor (omit if allergic)

½ cup unsweetened applesauce (or grated fresh apple)

¼ cup plain yogurt

1 teaspoon pure vanilla extract

2 tablespoons milk

1 large egg

2 tablespoons honey or pure maple syrup

¼ cup chocolate chips

Butter or cooking spray, for greasing skillet

Optional Extra Boost: ¼ cup fresh or frozen blueberries

Mix together Flour Blend, baking powder, salt, and ground almonds (optional). Set aside, if using immediately. (To store for later use, triple the dry ingredients and keep in a sealed, labeled plastic bag. You'll have instant pancake mix anytime you want it.)

In another bowl, whisk together the applesauce, yogurt, vanilla, milk, egg, and honey (or maple syrup) and optional blueberries, if desired. (If using frozen berries, don't thaw them before adding; this will prevent bleeding). Add the wet ingredients to the dry ones until just blended. If the batter is too thick, add a little more milk. Add the chocolate chips and mix lightly.

Butter or spray a large skillet over medium heat. Test the pan to see if it's hot enough by tossing a few drops of water in—it should sizzle. The skillet will grow hotter over time, so turn it down if it starts to smoke.

Drop tablespoons or small ladles of batter onto the skillet in batches. Try to get chocolate chips in with each pancake. When bubbles begin to set around the edges of the pancake and the skillet-side is golden (peek under), gently flip them over. Continue to cook 2 to 3 minutes or until the pancake is set.

Serve stacked high drizzled with warm maple syrup or, for an extra boost of fruit, Homemade Berry Syrup (see recipe, pg. 132).

According to a Harvard Medical School survey, children who eat breakfast do better academically and emotionally in school, resulting in better grades, behavior and attendance.

Cocoa Chocolate Chip Pancakes

Nutrition Highlights: Whole grains and fruit · Rich in vitamins A, C, E, and K, folate, iron, and fiber

It's hard to convince the mind that these chocolate pancakes are actually good for the body. I've been told that they taste like brownies, but rest assured they have more whole grains, fruit, and yes, even spinach, than breakfast at the health spa. They contain less sugar per serving than what I use in my morning tea, and the unsweetened cocoa in them not only hides the purple color of the pureed blueberries and spinach, but it is said to possess antidepressant qualities, something we all could use on cold winter mornings. My kids love them so much I put them in their lunch boxes and they eat them cold like soft cookies. Sometimes they even convince me to send a couple of dozen for the whole class!

MAKES ABOUT 18 PANCAKES

¾ cups Flour Blend (see Make-Ahead
   Recipe #13)

1 teaspoon baking powder

½ teaspoon salt

2 tablespoons unsweetened cocoa powder

1 teaspoon pure vanilla extract

¼ cup milk

1 large egg

¼ cup Purple Puree (see Make-Ahead
   Recipe #1)

2 tablespoons honey or pure maple syrup

¼ cup chocolate chips

Butter or cooking spray, for greasing skillet

Optional extra boost: ¼ cup fresh or frozen
   blueberries

Mix together Flour Blend, baking powder, salt, and cocoa powder. Set aside. (To store for instant cocoa pancake mix in the future, triple the dry ingredients and keep in a sealed, labeled plastic bag.) In another bowl, whisk together the vanilla, milk, egg, Purple Puree, honey (or maple syrup), and optional blueberries, if using. (If using frozen berries, don't thaw them before adding; this will prevent bleeding.) Add the wet ingredients to the dry ones until just blended. (Don't over-mix.) Add a little milk if batter is too thick. Add the chocolate chips and mix lightly.

Butter or spray a large skillet over medium heat. Test the pan to see if it's hot enough by tossing a few drops of water in — it should sizzle. The skillet will grow hotter over time, so turn it down if it starts to smoke. Drop tablespoons or small ladles of batter onto the skillet in batches. Try to get chocolate chips with each pancake. When bubbles begin to set around the edges of the pancake and the skillet-side of the pancake is golden (peek under), gently flip them over. Continue to cook 2 to 3 minutes or until pancakes are set.

Serve stacked high, dusted with powdered sugar, drizzled with warm maple syrup, or, for an extra boost of fruit, Homemade Berry Syrup (See recipe, pg. 132).

Kids who skip breakfast have a more than 250 percent increased risk for developing tooth decay, according to a study of more than 4,000 children aged 2 through 5 years published in the January 2004 Journal of the American Dental Association.

Homemade Berry Syrup

Nutrition Highlights: Fruit · Rich in vitamins A, C, and E, manganese, and antioxidants

There are subtle ways to add fruit to pancakes or waffles without having kids see them and then possibly object. You know kids, even if they like something, they don't always like it in combination with other things. Here, we get almost all of the rich nutrients of the fruit, mixed in with syrup, for a great tasting and fun dip.

MAKES ½ CUP OF SYRUP

¼ cup pure maple syrup

¼ cup Blueberry, Cherry, or Strawberry Juice (see Make-Ahead Recipe #6, 7, or 8)

Combine maple syrup and Juice. Serve warm.

Popeye's Eggs

Nutrition Highlights: Protein, vegetables, whole grains, and calcium · Rich in vitamins A and K, folate, iron, tryptophan, selenium, and calcium

*Here's a wacky recipe that goes really well with a breakfast reading of Dr. Seuss' **Green Eggs and Ham.** It's also a fun way to celebrate St. Patrick's Day or Earth Day. It's hard to believe, but the Green Juice leaves no discernable taste, only a terrific green color. This dish will either be a big hit with the kids or get you laughed out of the kitchen. You can also use the tortilla and cheese to hide the green eggs inside a breakfast wrap. The ham is strictly optional.*

MAKES 2 SMALL SERVINGS

Butter for pan

2 large eggs

¼ cup Green Juice (see Make-Ahead Recipe #5)

2 soft flour tortillas (preferably whole wheat)

2 slices American cheese (optional)

Salt

Melt butter in a small nonstick skillet over medium heat. Crack the eggs into a mixing bowl and whisk in the Green Juice until well incorporated. Add the beaten egg mixture to the skillet, allow to set briefly, and then, using a rubber spatula, lift edges of eggs as they cook, letting uncooked part run underneath until omelet is completely set.

Place half of the omelet in each tortilla, season with salt, and top each with a slice of cheese and roll up. The cheese will melt under the hot eggs.

If you prefer to serve these as scrambled eggs, simply pour the egg mixture into the hot skillet and stir frequently until they are cooked through.

Breakfast Ice Creams

Nutrition Highlights: Fruit, calcium, and probiotics

*The name alone makes kids giggle and school mornings go a bit smoother. Your kids will think you're the best when you call them into the kitchen for their morning "ice cream"! These two-minute recipes are fun enough to entice even the grumpiest kids. This is the **only** way I got my youngest daughter, Samantha, to eat anything in the morning all during her first year of kindergarten.*

*Your food processor is the only way to puree the frozen fruit without having to add a lot of liquid — and for these small quantities, a three-cup mini food processor works best. These recipes can be quickly converted to a thinner **smoothie** by adding an extra ½ cup of milk to all the variations below and then mixing them in the blender:*

EACH VARIATION BELOW SERVES 2 CHILDREN

Really Easy Strawberry Breakfast Ice Cream

Rich in vitamins C and K, potassium, folate, calcium, fiber, and protein

1½ cups frozen strawberries, without syrup or added sweeteners

½ cup milk

1 tablespoon honey or sugar

Extra Sneaky Strawberry Breakfast Ice Cream

Rich in vitamins C and K, potassium, folate, calcium, fiber and protein.

¼ ripe avocado

½ cup frozen strawberries, without syrup or added sweeteners

2 tablespoons plain yogurt

1 tablespoon honey or sugar

Banana Breakfast Ice Cream

Rich in vitamins B6, C, potassium, fiber, calcium, and protein

1 frozen banana, cut in pieces (about 1 cup)

2 tablespoons plain yogurt

1 tablespoon honey or sugar

Extra Sneaky Chocolate Breakfast Ice Cream

Rich in vitamins C and K, potassium, folate, calcium, fiber and protein

¼ ripe avocado

1 frozen banana, cut in pieces (about 1 cup)

2 tablespoons plain yogurt

1 tablespoon honey or sugar

½ teaspoon unsweetened cocoa powder

Chocolate Banana Breakfast Ice Cream

Rich in vitamins B6, C, potassium, fiber, calcium, protein, and antioxidants

1 frozen banana, cut in pieces (about 1 cup)

2 tablespoons plain yogurt

1 tablespoon honey or sugar

½ teaspoon unsweetened cocoa powder

Note: If you prefer to use sweetened yogurt (the vanilla flavored yogurt works well with all of the above), you probably won't need the extra sugar or honey.

For each of the above Breakfast Ice Creams, put all ingredients in food processor and puree on high — hold on tight, the first few seconds are a bit rough until the mixture smoothes out. Each makes about 1½ cups of ice cream.

Another sneaky hint: Make popsicles out of these ice creams by pouring them into ice pop molds and freezing them the night before. It's double the fun to eat it this way in the morning!

Fortified French Toast

Nutrition Highlights: Whole grains, protein, and vegetables · Rich in vitamins B, C, A, and K, potassium, fiber and calcium

I often make this batter the night before and leave it covered in the refrigerator for quicker french toast in the morning. The pureed sweet potatoes and carrots in the batter lend a hint of sweetness to the already delicious batter, and the optional crunchy topping is not only a great decoy technique, it adds whole grain health. If you don't have time for the topping, a light dusting of powdered sugar also does the trick.

MAKES 4 SLICES FRENCH TOAST

2 large eggs

½ cup milk

¼ cup Orange Puree (see Make-Ahead Recipe #2)

1 tablespoon pure maple syrup or honey

1 teaspoon cinnamon

1 teaspoon pure vanilla extract

4 slices bread (preferably whole wheat)

Butter for pan frying

Powdered sugar for dusting

In a large shallow baking dish, whisk together the eggs, milk, Orange Puree, maple syrup (or honey), cinnamon, and vanilla. Dip bread until soaked through, then flip and soak other side. Cook on a moderately hot, well-greased skillet or frying pan, turning to brown each side. Dust lightly with powdered sugar.

French Toast Dip Sticks

Following the preceding recipe, cut the pieces of french toast into kid-friendly finger-sized sticks so that they can dip them into maple syrup or Homemade Berry Syrup (see recipe, pg. 132).

Crunchy French Toast Variation

1 cup whole grain cereal flakes (like Wheaties or Total)

¼ cup wheat germ, unsweetened

Using a rolling pin, gently crush cereal (in a sealed plastic bag) to coarse crushed flakes. Alternatively, you can quickly pulse the cereal in a food processor. Pour crushed cereal on a plate, and add the wheat germ. Mix well. Dip each side of the soaked bread from the above recipe in the topping. Proceed to pan fry in butter as instructed.

Sneaky Tip:

Smell eggs after cracking to be sure there is no "off" odor.

Quick Fixes for Oatmeal

*Oatmeal is a good food to start with, but can be made even better with some simple tweaking. First, always begin with "old-fashioned" rolled oats, not the "quick cooking" version. They are nearly as fast to make and provide more fiber and longer-lasting energy. Then, you can add more fiber and nutrients by adding in any or all of the following boosters to ¹/₂ **cup of dry oats:***

---

* 1 cup milk

Rich in calcium

Simply substitute milk for water when cooking oatmeal.

* 1 to 3 teaspoons wheat germ

Rich in vitamin B and E, iron, potassium, folic acid, and protein

Make oatmeal according to package directions, adding wheat germ with the oats. You may need to add a bit more liquid if the oatmeal seems too dry.

* 1 to 3 teaspoons oat bran

Rich in vitamins B, manganese, selenium, and fiber

Make oatmeal according to package directions, adding oat bran with the oats. You may need to add a bit more liquid if the oatmeal seems too dry.

* 1 cup Blueberry, Cherry, or Strawberry Juice
(see Make-Ahead Recipes #6, 7, or 8)

Rich in vitamins A, C, E, manganese, antioxidants, and fiber

Simply substitute juice for water when cooking oatmeal.

* 1 to 3 teaspoons blanched, slivered almonds, ground in a food processor

Rich in vitamin E, manganese, tryptophan, magnesium, and fiber

Make oatmeal according to package directions, adding ground almonds with the oats. You may need to add a bit more liquid if the oatmeal seems too dry.

* 1 to 3 tablespoons nonfat dry milk

Prepare oatmeal according to directions on package. Mix dry milk into the oatmeal, mixing until well blended.

Breakfast Cookies and Milk

Nutrition Highlights: Whole grains, calcium, and protein · Rich in vitamins B and E, iron, potassium, folic acid, calcium, tryptophan protein, and fiber

Finally, a healthy cookie that doesn't taste like the box it came in. This is a high-protein cookie with plenty of whole grain carbs to keep kids going for hours, and contains less than half the sugar of kids' breakfast cereals (approximately 6 grams of sugar per large cookie, compared to at least 12 grams in most cereals). I make these on the weekend, freeze them in a large plastic bag, and grab a couple whenever I'm on my way out the door. They're fast, healthy, and deliciously kid-approved.

MAKES 16 TO 18 LARGE COOKIES

2 cups whole grain cereal flakes (such as Wheaties or Total)

¾ cup Flour Blend (see Make-Ahead Recipe #13)

½ teaspoon baking soda

½ teaspoon salt

1 teaspoon cinnamon

1 large egg

½ cup brown sugar

¼ cup canola oil

2 teaspoons pure vanilla extract

¾ cup low-fat ricotta cheese

Cinnamon sugar for dusting

Preheat oven to 400 degrees and line a baking sheet with parchment paper (or spray with oil).

Using a rolling pin, gently crush the cereal (in a sealed plastic bag) into coarsely crushed flakes. Alternatively, you can quickly pulse the cereal in a food processor.

In a large mixing bowl, whisk together Flour Blend, crushed cereal, baking soda, salt and cinnamon. In another bowl, whisk together egg, sugar, oil, vanilla, and ricotta cheese. Add the dry ingredients to the wet and mix just enough to moisten dry ingredients. Drop single tablespoonfuls onto the baking sheets, leaving about an inch between cookies. Flatten cookies with the back of a fork and then sprinkle tops generously with cinnamon sugar (or just sugar if your kids don't like the cinnamon flavor). Bake about 18 to 20 minutes, or until nicely browned and crispy around the edges.

Serve with Flavored Milk, page 254, or Cheery Hot Cocoa, page 257.

Cinnamon has been found to help stabilize blood-glucose levels, thereby preventing the usual "crash and burn" feeling we all get after eating sweets.

Peanut Butter and Jelly Muffins

Nutrition Highlights: Vegetables, whole grains, nuts · Rich in vitamins A, B complex, C, E, and K, manganese, iron, potassium, folate, riboflavin, selenium, fiber, and protein

My friend Alison came over one day and saw the sneaky puree of sweet potatoes and carrots out on my counter. "Yuck, I hate sweet potatoes," she screeched, sounding worse than a kid. As she pushed away the puree with one hand, she grabbed a freshly-made peanut butter muffin off the counter with the other hand and chomped into it before I could warn her what was in it. "Yum," she squealed, "these are great!" She was astounded when I told her that they had sweet potatoes in them, and it definitely didn't stop her from gobbling down the rest of the muffin. Case closed.

MAKES 8 LARGE MUFFINS (OR 16 MINI MUFFINS)

1 cup Flour Blend (See Make-Ahead
  Recipe #13)

2 teaspoons baking powder

½ teaspoon baking soda

½ teaspoon salt

2 large eggs

¼ cup brown sugar

¼ cup canola oil

¾ cup Orange Puree (see Make-Ahead
  Recipe #2)

¾ cup smooth peanut butter

8 heaping teaspoons favorite jam*

Note: Jelly doesn't work as well as the thicker variety of jam; jelly just disappears into the muffins.

Preheat oven to 350 degrees and line a muffin tin with paper liners.

In a mixing bowl, whisk together the Flour Blend, baking powder, baking soda and salt; set aside. In another large bowl, whisk together the eggs and sugar until well combined, then whisk in the oil, Orange Puree, and peanut butter. Fold the dry ingredients into the wet and mix until flour is just moistened (don't over-mix or the muffins will be dense).

Scoop about two tablespoons of batter into the large muffin cups until half full. Place a heaping teaspoon of jam in the center of each muffin. Cover the jam with another 2 tablespoons or so of batter, filling the cups just over the top. If you're using mini-muffin cups, scale back quantities to fit into the smaller sized cups.

Bake for 25 to 30 minutes, until the tops are golden brown.

Complete Corn Muffins

Nutrition Highlights: Vegetables and whole grains · Rich in vitamins B, C, E, and K, iron, potassium, selenium, tryptophan, manganese, riboflavin, folate, protein, and fiber

I use a few chocolate chips on top as a lure to get the kids to eat these whole grain, three-veggie corn muffins. The chocolate does the trick every time. Or for cheese lovers, sprinkle a little shredded cheddar on the tops before baking for a quick conversion to bubbly, cheesy muffins.

MAKES 6 LARGE MUFFINS (OR 12 MINI-MUFFINS)

½ cup Flour Blend (See Make-Ahead Recipe #13)

½ cup yellow cornmeal

2 teaspoons baking powder

½ teaspoon baking soda

½ teaspoon salt

2 large eggs

¼ cup brown sugar

¼ cup canola oil

½ cup White Puree (See Make-Ahead Recipe #4)

½ cup fresh or frozen corn kernels, pureed

Optional toppings: ¼ cup chocolate chips or ¼ cup shredded low-fat cheese

Preheat oven to 350 degrees and line a muffin tin with paper liners.

In a mixing bowl, whisk together the Flour Blend, cornmeal, baking powder, baking soda, and salt. In another large bowl, whisk together the eggs and sugar until well combined, then whisk in the oil, White Puree, and pureed corn. Fold the wet ingredients into the dry and mix until flour is just moistened (don't over-mix or the muffins will be dense).

Scoop the batter into muffin tins, filling just over the top. If you're using mini-muffin cups, scale back quantities to fit into the smaller sized cups. Top with a few chocolate chips, or sprinkle with shredded cheese, and bake for 22 to 24 minutes until tops are golden brown and a toothpick inserted in the center comes out clean.

Grilled Cheese Muffins

Nutrition Highlights: Vegetables, calcium, whole grains, and protein · Rich in vitamins A, B complex, C, E, and K, iron, potassium, manganese, riboflavin, folate, selenium, and tryptophan

The bubbly, cheesy tops on these muffins look so sinful and decadent they'll make you ask, "Where's the wheat germ?" These muffins are every bit as nutritious as their ugly stepsister, the traditional carrot bran muffin, with at least two huge advantages: they look and taste great, and you can actually get these into most grilled-cheese loving kids.

MAKES 8 LARGE MUFFINS (OR 16 MINI MUFFINS)

1 cup Flour Blend (see Make-Ahead Recipe #13)

2 teaspoons baking powder

½ teaspoon baking soda

½ teaspoon salt

¼ cup grated Parmesan cheese

1 cup grated low-fat cheddar cheese (save ¼ cup for tops)

2 large eggs

3 tablespoons brown sugar

¼ cup canola oil

¾ cup Orange Puree (see Make-Ahead Recipe #2)

Preheat oven to 350 degrees and line a muffin tin with paper liners.

In a mixing bowl, whisk together the Flour Blend, baking powder, baking soda, and salt. Add the Parmesan and ¾ cup of the cheddar cheese and set aside. In another large bowl, whisk together the eggs and sugar until well combined, then whisk in the oil and Orange Puree. Fold the wet ingredients into the dry and mix until flour is just moistened (don't over-mix or the muffins will be dense).

Scoop the batter into muffin tins, filling just over the top. If you're using mini muffin cups, scale back quantities to fit into the smaller sized cups. Sprinkle the tops evenly with the remaining ¼ cup of cheese and bake for 25 to 30 minutes until tops are golden brown and a toothpick inserted in the center comes out clean.

Serve muffins warm.

LUNCH RECIPES

Masterful Mac 'n' Cheese

Nutrition Highlights: Whole grains, calcium, and vegetables · Rich in vitamins C, folate, manganese, calcium, protein, and fiber.

This is a nutritionally enhanced version of my stepmother's delicious recipe from Finland. When I mixed in the cauliflower/zucchini puree, which melted away in the familiar creaminess of the cheese, the kids didn't notice any difference from the original mac 'n' cheese. Another great distraction is the crunchy topping, which not only adds a good dose of whole grains, but also became my kids' favorite part of the casserole. Start at ¼ cup of the White Puree in this recipe and gradually increase it to ½ cup over time.

MAKES 4 TO 6 SERVINGS

½ pound macaroni (preferably whole wheat blend)

1½ cups milk

¼ to ½ cup White Puree (See Make-Ahead Recipe #4)

½ teaspoon salt

2 cups grated low-fat colby or cheddar cheese

Optional Extra boost: 2 large eggs

Preheat oven to 375 degrees. Butter a 9-inch square baking pan.

Bring a large pot of salted water to a boil over high heat. Add the macaroni and cook according to the package directions, until firm and slightly undercooked. Drain and set aside.

In a large bowl, whisk the milk with the White Puree and salt. (If using eggs, whisk them in with the milk mixture.) Put half of the macaroni into the baking pan and top with half the cheddar (or colby) cheese. Next, layer with the rest of the macaroni, and then pour the milk mixture over the top, finishing with the last of the cheese on top.

Orange Puree Variation

Follow exact instructions above for Masterful Mac 'n Cheese, replacing the White Puree with Orange Puree (see Make-Ahead Recipe #2)

Crunchy Topping Variation

1 cup whole grain cereal flakes (like Wheaties or Total)

¼ cup wheat germ, unsweetened

2 tablespoons grated Parmesan

2 tablespoons butter, diced into small pieces

Using a rolling pin, gently crush cereal (in a sealed plastic plastic bag) to coarsely crushed flakes. Alternatively, you can quickly pulse the cereal in a food processor. Add wheat germ and Parmesan to the bag and shake to mix. Sprinkle crumb mixture on top of macaroni and cheese and dot with butter.

Bake casserole 30 to 35 minutes, or until golden and bubbling.

Quick Fixes for Boxed Macaroni and Cheese

There's not a kids' menu in the United States that doesn't offer some variation of macaroni and cheese—the favorite of American comfort foods. Kraft now sells more than one million boxes every day! For the purposes of this book, the beauty of even the packaged version is that its cheesy creaminess offers ample opportunity for sneaky chefs to slip in extra nutrition that even the toughest little critics won't detect. Try to keep a straight face as your kids beg for more of these surprisingly healthy variations.

Note: Yellow macaroni and cheese usually contains yellow food dye, whereas the white version does not. If your child insists on yellow, you can add a slice of yellow American or cheddar cheese and a dash of paprika to the white cheese sauce, which will help safely change the color to yellow without affecting the taste.

All of the nutritional boosters listed here have been kid tested and have proven to be undetectable in taste, texture and color. Start by adding the least amount recommended of just one of the nutritional boosters listed below. Add a little more each time you serve this dish (which is served in our house almost every day!). You can also mix two or more of the boosters as long as the total is no more than about half cup total of puree per six ounce box of macaroni and cheese.

* 2 to 4 tablespoons White Bean Puree
   (See Make-Ahead Recipe #9)

Prepare macaroni and cheese according to directions on package. Add pureed white beans into the cheese sauce, mixing until well blended.

* 2 to 4 tablespoons White Puree

    (see Make-Ahead Recipe #4)

Prepare macaroni and cheese according to directions on package. Add White Puree into the cheese sauce, mixing until well blended. If sauce becomes too dry, simply add an extra tablespoon of milk and extra cheese (See below).

* 2 to 4 tablespoons Orange Puree

    (See Make-Ahead Recipe #2)

Prepare macaroni and cheese according to directions on package. Add Orange Puree into the cheese sauce, mixing until well blended. This one works best with an extra slice of American cheese or ¼ cup of grated low-fat cheddar melted into the sauce to help mask the carrots in the puree.

Note: These may not seem like large quantities to you, but if you use the recipes in this book consistently, you will be feeding your kids a little here and a little there. Over time, it adds up. Also, don't forget that these are concentrated doses of nutrients.

¼ cup to ½ cup tofu

Prepare macaroni and cheese according to directions on package. Puree tofu in a food processor until smooth or mash it well with the back of a fork. Add pureed tofu into the cheese sauce, mixing until well blended.

* 1 to 2 slices American cheese or ¼ cup

    grated low-fat cheddar cheese

Prepare macaroni and cheese according to directions on package. Add extra cheese to the packaged cheese sauce, mixing well until completely melted.

Guerilla Grilled Cheese

Nutrition Highlights: Whole grains, calcium, and vegetables · Rich in vitamins A, K, and C, manganese, potassium, fiber, and calcium

Guerrilla tactics are at work here in this subtly upgraded grilled cheese. The addition of heart-healthy olive oil cuts the amount of butter needed, and the addition of pureed orange vegetables adds a layer of nutrition that hides beneath the orange cheese.

MAKES 2 SANDWICHES

4 teaspoons butter

4 teaspoons extra virgin olive oil

4 teaspoons Orange Puree (See Make-Ahead Recipe #2)

4 slices yellow American cheese

4 slices bread, preferably whole wheat

> **"Extra Virgin Olive Oil"** — the oil from the first pressing of the olives — contains higher levels of antioxidants and vitamin E than regular olive oil.

Melt 1 teaspoon of butter with 1 teaspoon of the olive oil in a small skillet over medium-low heat. Spread 1 teaspoon of Orange Puree in the center of each slice of bread, staying away from the edges (to keep the puree from oozing out). Top each side of the bread with 2 slices of cheese, close sandwiches, and place 1 sandwich in the skillet. Cook, without pressing, about 3 to 4 minutes until the bread is golden. Flip sandwich, adding another teaspoon each of the butter and oil to the pan, and brown the other side, about 3 to 4 minutes more.

Repeat with the other sandwich. Let cool for a few minutes before cutting.

Quick Fixes for Tuna Fish Sandwiches

*Any or all of the ingredients listed below hide beautifully in a 6-ounce can of **chunk light*** *or chunk white tuna, packed in water and drained. As with all Sneaky Chef recipes, you can gradually increase the amount of the nutritious sneaky ingredient over time. You can also combine any or all of the following Quick Fixes.*

"Chunk white" tuna contains up to three times the harmful mercury of "chunk light" tuna. Try to get your child used to the chunk light variety as soon as possible.

---

* Canned skinless and boneless sardines in water:

Sardines have almost no mercury and lots of IQ-boosting omega-3 oils. Mixing them in with the tuna fish your kids already love gives them an instant nutritional boost. Start by mixing in 2 ounces of sardines per 6 ounces of tuna, and over time, gradually increase the amount of sardines until there are equal parts sardines and tuna (or even more sardines, eventually — this *is* possible!). Continue to stir in mayonnaise or whatever you normally add to your child's tuna fish.

* White Bean Puree (see Make-Ahead Recipe #9):

Combine 1 tablespoon of White Bean Puree with every 1 tablespoon of mayonnaise for tuna salad.

* Wheat Germ:

Start by mixing in 1 tablespoon of wheat germ per 6-ounce can of tuna, along with mayonnaise (and White Bean Puree if desired), and, over time, gradually increase to 2 tablespoons of wheat germ.

IQ Tuna Patties

Nutrition Highlights: Whole grains, protein, beans, and omega-3s · Rich in vitamin E, omega-3 fatty acids, fiber, folate, manganese, and protein

Your kids will love these pan-fried tuna patties and never know about your healthy additions.

MAKES 4 TO 6 PATTIES

1 can (6 ounce) Chunk Light Tuna, packed in water, drained

1 can (3 to 4 ounce) skinless and boneless sardines, packed in water, drained

1 large egg

3 tablespoons White Bean Puree (See Make-Ahead Recipe #9)

1 tablespoon mayonnaise

2 teaspoons fresh lemon juice

3 tablespoons wheat germ

¼ teaspoon salt

2 tablespoons olive oil for pan frying

Optional extra boost: ½ cup diced celery and/or ½ cup grated carrot

Combine tuna, sardines, egg, White Bean Puree, mayonnaise, lemon juice, wheat germ, salt, and celery or carrot (if using). Shape tuna mixture into 4 to 6 patties. In a large nonstick fry pan, heat oil over medium heat. Pan fry for 4 to 5 minutes on each side or until cooked through and lightly browned on both sides.

If desired, serve on whole grain hamburger buns or English muffins.

Crunchy Variation

Make the patties above and then add this delicious topping.

1 cup whole grain cereal flakes (such as Wheaties or Total)

¼ cup wheat germ, unsweetened

2 tablespoons grated parmesan

Using a rolling pin, gently crush cereal (in a sealed plastic bag) into coarsely crushed flakes. Alternatively, you can quickly pulse the cereal in a food processor. Pour crushed cereal on a plate, and add the wheat germ and parmesan. Mix well. Dip tuna patties in the dry mix on each side, then pan fry in olive oil as instructed above.

A study by the University of Adelaide in Australia found that fish oil improves the symptoms of attention deficit hyperactivity disorder (ADHD) without any of the side effects of drugs like Ritalin and Concerta.

Sneaky Tip:

When buying fresh fish, especially salmon, try to choose "wild" over "farmed" fish. It contains fewer PCBs and lower mercury levels.

Packed Pizza Bagels

Nutrition Highlights: Whole grains, vegetables, beans, and calcium · Rich in vitamins A, C, and K, folate, potassium, iron, fiber, and calcium

Pizza lovers rejoiced when researchers announced the results of a study indicating that "people who ate pizza several times a week were less likely to get cancer of the digestive tract than those who did not eat pizza at all." What a great excuse to wolf down pizza! For added insurance, these mini pizza bagels are made even healthier by the injection of carrots, yams, and white beans, all of which hide quietly under the blanket of bubbly cheese.

I prepare these little treats, without cooking them, and then refrigerate them for a day or two. They're fast and easy to pop into the toaster oven when the kids get home from school.

MAKES 8 HALF PIZZA BAGELS

½ cup store-bought tomato sauce (or ¾ cup Easy Homemade Pasta Sauce*, pg. 208)

¼ cup White Bean Puree (see Make-Ahead Recipe #9)

3 tablespoons Orange Puree (see Make-Ahead Recipe #2)

4 mini bagels, sliced in half (preferably whole wheat)

1 cup grated part-skim mozzarella cheese

if using Easy Homemade Pasta Sauce, then omit the additional Orange Puree in this recipe.

Combine tomato sauce with White Bean Puree and Orange Puree. Mix well. Spread 1 tablespoon of sauce on each bagel half and then top with 1 tablespoon of grated cheese without covering the hole. Cover and refrigerate at this point, or toast on high for 5 to 6 minutes until cheese is melted and bubbly.

Quick Fixes for SpaghettiOs

Each of the nutritional boosters listed below has been kid-tested and has proven to be undetectable in taste, texture, and color. Start by adding the least amount recommended of just one of the following nutritional boosters, and then put in a little more every time you serve this dish. You can also mix two or more of the boosters below, up to about a half cup total per 15-ounce can of SpaghettiOs (or a similar, more natural product, like Annie's Organic canned pasta meals).

2 to 4 tablespoons White Bean Puree (see Make-Ahead Recipe #9)

Combine White Bean Puree and SpaghettiOs (or another canned pasta meal) in a pot and warm, mixing until well blended.

2 to 4 tablespoons White Puree (see Make-Ahead Recipe #4)

Combine White Puree and SpaghettiOs (or another canned pasta meal) in a pot and warm, mixing until well blended.

2 to 4 tablespoons Orange Puree (see Make-Ahead Recipe #2)

Combine Orange Puree and SpaghettiOs (or another canned pasta meal) in a pot and warm, mixing until well blended.

Pigs in Healthy Blankets

Nutrition Highlights: Whole grains, vegetables, calcium, and protein · Rich in vitamins A, B, C, E and K, iron, folate, manganese, fiber, and protein

What better place to hide healthy stuff than under a yummy blanket? These cheesy dogs essentially have their bun baked right on, giving sneaky chefs the opportunity to add an extra layer of whole grains and pureed veggies. If your children don't like cheese with hot dogs, simply skip down to the no cheese variation below. These fun dogs are also great for parties and play dates. You can prepare them up to a day in advance and cook when ready to serve.

MAKES 8 SANDWICHES

- 3 tablespoons wheat germ, unsweetened
- 6 tablespoons White (or Orange) Puree (see Make-Ahead #4 or 2)
- 1 store bought pizza dough (preferably whole wheat)
- 8 slices American cheese
- 8 hot dogs, turkey or beef (preferably with no nitrates)

Note: You can use both Orange and White Puree in this recipe; just reduce the amount to 3 tablespoons of each.

Preheat oven to 375 degrees. Spray a baking sheet with oil.

In a bowl, mix the wheat germ and White (or Orange) Puree. Tear off 8 small handfuls of dough and spread them into approximately 6-inch circles. Alternatively, you can roll out dough balls with a floured rolling pin on a floured surface to approximately 6-inch circles. Spread about a tablespoon of the puree mixture in the center of each circle, leaving about a 1-inch border with no puree (so that it doesn't ooze out during cooking). Lay a slice of cheese on top of the puree, then add a hot dog and roll up. The ends of the hot dog can stick out of the dough a little. Place sandwiches (seam-side down so that they don't unroll) on your prepared baking sheet and spray the tops of the sandwiches with oil.

Bake for 15 to 20 minutes until golden brown. Let cool for at least 5 minutes, as the center is very hot.

White Bean Puree Variation

Follow exact instructions for Pigs in Healthy Blankets, but replace the White (or Orange) Puree with the same amount of White Bean Puree (See Make-Ahead Recipe #9).

No Cheese Variation

Follow exact instructions for Pigs in Healthy Blankets, but use only the wheat germ and White Puree (*not* the Orange Puree) and omit the cheese slices.

Warning: Hot dogs are a choking hazard for children under 4.

Franks 'n' Beans

Nutrition Highlights: beans, protein, and vegetables · Rich in vitamins A, C, and K, iron, manganese, fiber folate, tryptophan, magnesium, and protein

This recipe couldn't be faster or easier and combines most kids' favorites—hot dogs and baked beans. The yams and carrots in the Orange Puree add not only a top source of nutrients and fiber but a delicious hint of sweetness.

MAKES 4 SERVINGS

4 hot dogs, turkey or beef (preferably with no nitrates), sliced

1 can (approximately 16 ounces) baked beans

½ cup Orange Puree (see Make-Ahead Recipe #2)

1 tablespoon ketchup

Put the hot dogs, beans, Orange Puree, and ketchup in a saucepan and heat over medium until heated through, about 10 minutes, stirring occasionally. Alternatively, place ingredients in microwave-safe bowl, cover the top of the bowl with a wet paper towel, and microwave on high for 3 to 4 minutes, pausing to stir occasionally.

Warning: Hot dogs are a choking hazard for children under 4.

A note about the food photos on the following pages: All of the food you see on the next several pages were made exactly according to the recipes in this book, under the watchful eye of the author. Whereas food styling and food photography often uses trickery and substitutes to stretch the truth and make the food look more appealing, this was definitely not the case here. What you see is what you get! The wonderful team of the stylist, chef, and photographer remained true to every ingredient in the book, using all the sneaky purees and ingredients. It's hard to believe it when you see these photos of decadent looking food, but every one of the following fruits and veggies are all in there!

MAC 'N' CHEESE

Sneaky Ingredients: Cauliflower, Zucchini, Yams, Carrots

MILKSHAKES

Sneaky Ingredients:

Spinach

Avocado

Blueberries

OVEN FRIED DRUMSTICKS

Sneaky Ingredients:

Whole grain cereal

Wheat germ

Cauliflower

Zucchini

SAY YES
TO SORBET

Sneaky Ingredients:

Blueberries

Cherries

Strawberries

Pomegranate Juice

POWER PIZZA

Sneaky Ingredients:

Yams

Carrots

Cauliflower

Zucchini

Tomatoes

White beans

Whole grain crust

GOTTA LOTTA LASAGNA

Sneaky Ingredients:

Tofu

Cauliflower

Zucchini

Tomatoes

PEANUT BUTTER AND JELLY MUFFINS

Sneaky Ingredients:

Yams

Carrots

Wheat germ

Whole grain flour

ROYAL ICE POPS

Sneaky Ingredients:

Blueberries

Cherries

Strawberries

CHOCOLATE
CHIP PANCAKES

Sneaky Ingredients:

Whole grain flour

Wheat germ

Applesauce

Yogurt

Almonds (optional)

MAGIC MEATBALLS (AND SAUCE)

Sneaky Ingredients:

Broccoli

Spinach

Peas

Tomatoes

Wheat germ

Yams

Carrots

Cauliflower

Zucchini

CHOC-FUL CUPCAKES AND INCREDIBLY IMPROVED ICING

Sneaky Ingredients:

Blueberries

Spinach

Wheat germ

Whole grain flour

Nonfat dry milk

UNBELIEVABLE CHOCOLATE CHIP COOKIES

Sneaky Ingredients:

White beans

Wheat germ

Whole grain flour

Oats

Almonds (optional)

CRUNCHY CHICKEN TENDERS

Sneaky Ingredients:

Yams

Carrots

Wheat germ

Whole grain bread crumbs

**EXTRA SNEAKY
CHOCOLATE
BANANA
BREAKFAST
ICE CREAM**

Sneaky Ingredients:

Avocado

Bananas

Yogurt

**BRAINY
BROWNIES**

Sneaky Ingredients:

Blueberries

Spinach

Wheat germ

Whole grain flour

Oats

Creative Cream of Tomato Soup

Nutrition Highlights: Vegetables, protein, calcium, and fiber · Rich in vitamins A, C, and K, lycopene, manganese and fiber

*Evaporated skim milk is a terrific low-fat technique, I learned while working at **Eating Well** maga-zine, in addition to being a sneaky healthy ingredient. It is concentrated and has a consistency similar to cream, providing twice the amount of calcium and protein as the same amount of regular milk and it replaces fattening heavy cream. The yams and carrots add a subtle sweetness to this soup, as well as a terrific boost of nutrition, and help cut the acidity of the tomato. If you're feeling extra ambitious, add ¼ cup of White Bean Puree (See Make-Ahead Recipe #9), which makes this soup a meal in a bowl and adds extra fiber, protein, and vitamins.*

MAKES 2 SERVINGS

1 can (10 ¾ ounces) tomato soup, condensed

1 ½ cups evaporated skim milk*

¼ cup Orange Puree (See Make-Ahead Recipe #2)

*If you choose a tomato soup that is not condensed and doesn't require additional liquid, simply reduce the amount of evaporated milk to a few tablespoons or so.

Cook all of the ingredients on the stovetop over medium heat for about 5 minutes, stirring occasionally. Alternatively, place ingredients in microwave-safe bowl, cover the top of the bowl with a wet paper towel, and microwave on high for 3 to 4 minutes, pausing to stir occasionally.

Creamy Chicken Noodle Soup

Nutrition Highlights: protein, beans and vegetables (optional) · Rich in vitamin B, iron, tryptophan, selenium, magnesium, folate, manganese, protein, and fiber

As delicious as cream soups are, they're among the first luxuries to go when following a healthier lifestyle. You can welcome the creamy decadence back into your family with this deceptive recipe. Here again, I substituted evaporated low-fat milk for heavy cream, which not only adds a concentrated dose of calcium but also offers a rich, creamy taste without the fat. The White Bean Puree and tiny bit of butter and flour also help to make a nice rich soup, while adding a dose of fiber and B vitamins.

Naturally, the optional extra vegetables are a plus here, but if your children object, then omit and go with the simple creamy chicken noodle soup.

MAKES ABOUT 4 SERVINGS

1 tablespoon butter

1 tablespoon **white** flour

2 cups chicken broth, homemade or
  low-sodium canned/boxed (no MSG)

¼ cup White Bean Puree (See Make-Ahead
  Recipe #9)

¼ cup cooked egg noodles or macaroni

1 cup diced, cooked chicken meat

¼ cup evaporated low-fat milk

Salt to taste

Optional extra boost: **diced celery, carrots
  and/or parsnips**

Melt the butter in a soup pot over medium heat. Sprinkle the flour over the butter and stir constantly for a minute with a wooden spoon (this is a roux, a fancy name for a thickener). Pour in the broth and mix in the White Bean Puree pasta. If you are adding any optional vegetables, do so at this point. Lower the heat and simmer for 10 to 15 minutes or until the vegetables are soft. Stir in the cooked chicken, cooked pasta, and the evaporated milk, mixing for a minute. Remove from heat and serve.

Sneaky Tip:

Never heat food in the microwave using plastic containers or plastic wrap. This especially applies to foods that contain fat. The combination of fat, high heat and plastics releases dioxins (chemicals that can cause cancer) into the food. Instead, use glass, Pyrex, or ceramic dishes in the microwave and cover food with a wet paper towel instead.

Tricky Taco Soup

Nutrition Highlights: vegetables, protein, calcium, and fiber · Rich in vitamins A, C, and K, lycopene, manganese, and fiber

Soup makes my job as a sneaky chef so much easier. You can puree healthy stuff to your heart's content and keep adding it to the pot. We've stopped at pureed white beans, yams, and carrots, but feel free to keep going. This soup is intentionally mild for children, but I added some chopped chipotle chiles to give my husband's portion a nice kick.

MAKES 6 TO 8 SERVINGS

1 tablespoon extra virgin olive oil

1 medium onion, pureed or very finely chopped

2 (4-ounce) cans tomato paste

½ cup mild salsa*

¼ cup Orange Puree (See Make-Ahead Recipe #2)

¼ cup White Bean Puree (See Make-Ahead Recipe #9)

4 cups chicken broth, homemade or low-sodium canned/boxed (no MSG)

1 pound chicken meat, cooked and shredded

2 teaspoons fresh lime juice

Salt and pepper to taste

Optional garnishes: crumbled tortilla chips, shredded cheddar, low-fat sour cream, corn

Sneaky Tip:

If salsa is too chunky and you think that might cause kids to object, just puree it in the food processor before mixing it into the soup.

Goes well with Crunchy Corn Chips, page 178, and No Doc Guac, page 183.

Heat oil over medium in a soup pot or Dutch oven. Cook the onions until they are slightly translucent, and then add the tomato paste, salsa, and Orange and White Bean purees, and stir for a minute. Add the chicken broth and bring to a simmer for 10 to 15 minutes, stirring occasionally. Add the chicken and simmer for another few minutes. Add the lime juice and season with salt and pepper to taste. Remove from heat and ladle soup into individual bowls.

Place the garnishes on the table in separate bowls. Let the children top their soup with whatever garnishes they desire. They're more likely to eat when they help prepare the food themselves.

Covert Quesadillas

Nutrition Highlights: Vegetables, calcium, and whole grains • Rich in vitamins A, B1 (thiamin), C, E, and K, folate, potassium, tryptophan, fiber and calcium (added benefit: no gluten)

Any sandwich that virtually seals itself shut is a good hiding place for the sneaky chef. The cheese acts as a great texture and flavor decoy for our hidden purees, and if your children will eat chicken, skip right down to the chicken variation and make a full meal out of this fun Mexican grilled cheese.

MAKES 6 QUESADILLAS

12 (6-inch) round corn tortillas, white or yellow

¼ to ½ cup Orange Puree (See Make-Ahead Recipe #2)

1½ cups low-fat shredded cheddar cheese (or 12 slices American cheese)

6 teaspoons extra virgin olive oil

Place all 12 tortillas on your work surface and spread 1 to 2 teaspoons of Orange Puree on each and every tortilla, being careful to keep puree away from the edges (leave about a 1-inch border so that it doesn't ooze out during cooking). Add about ½ cup of shredded cheese (or 2 cheese slices) to the center of just 6 of the tortillas and cover with the remaining tortillas to make 6 sandwiches. Heat 1 teaspoon of oil in a skillet over medium heat until hot but not smoking. Place one quesadilla in the heated skillet and cook until underside is lightly browned and cheese melts, about 2 to 3 minutes. Gently flip quesadilla and cook until the other side is golden, another 2 to 3 minutes. Add another teaspoon of oil and repeat with each of the remaining quesadillas.

Stack finished quesadillas on a plate with a paper towel between each sandwich to absorb excess oil. Allow to cool for a few minutes and then cut each sandwich into 4 triangles.

White Bean Puree Variation

Rich in vitamins B1 (Thiamin) and E, folate, calcium, potassium, tryptophan, manganese, magnesium, iron, fiber and protein

Follow instructions for Covert Quesadillas, but replace the Orange Puree with the same amount of White Bean Puree (See Make-Ahead Recipe #9).

Chicken Quesadilla Variation

Additional ingredient: 2 cups shredded cooked chicken (about 6 ounces)

Follow instructions for Covert Quesadillas (either Orange Puree or White Bean Puree variation) and add about 1 ounce of cooked chicken on top of the cheese (or between cheese slices) in each quesadilla. Proceed to pan fry as directed above.

All variations go well with No Doc Guac on page 183, and Tricky Taco Soup on page 192.

Sneaky Tip:

Scissors are the easiest way to cut quesadillas.

Crunchy Elbows

Nutrition Highlights: Whole grains, calcium, and nuts (optional) · Rich in vitamins B and E, iron, riboflavin, potassium, folic acid, calcium, protein, and fiber

This sounds (and tastes) decadent, but it's actually much healthier than the plain white pasta with butter that kids normally eat. For every half-cup serving of pasta, there's less than a teaspoon of butter and some heart-healthy olive oil, served up with a good amount of whole grains and fiber. Whole wheat macaroni is ideal, but don't worry if your child prefers white macaroni for this dish because the wheat germ, whole grain breadcrumbs, and ground almonds in the Better Breading add fiber and B vitamins.

This recipe can be made from leftover or freshly made pasta and works just as well with little shells or any small pasta.

MAKES 4 TO 6 SERVINGS

2 tablespoons extra virgin olive oil

1 tablespoon butter

3 cups cooked macaroni (whole wheat preferred)

½ teaspoon salt

½ cup Better Breading (See Make-Ahead Recipe #12)

¼ cup grated Parmesan cheese

Heat oil and butter over medium-high heat in a large skillet. Add the macaroni and salt, allow to brown (but not burn) for a minute, then stir to toast all sides. Cook for about 5 minutes, stirring occasionally, until macaroni is lightly browned and crispy. Reduce heat to medium and add Better Breading and parmesan cheese. Stir frequently for another few minutes until nicely toasted. Serve warm.

SNACKS

Crunchy Corn Chips

Nutrition Highlights: Whole grains and calcium · Rich in vitamins E and B1 (thiamin), folate, calcium, potassium, and fiber (added benefit: no gluten)

*After seeing how fast, fun, and easy these chips are to make, you'll wonder why anyone buys the kind in the bag. Not only are these crunchy snacks not **bad** for kids, they are also actually **good** for them, providing a good source of calcium, iron, and fiber, all for a fraction of the calories and fat of packaged tortilla chips. These chips are so tasty they probably won't make it off the cookie sheet and into the bowl before most of them are eaten. You can easily vary the shapes by cutting strips instead of triangles, to keep things interesting and new.*

MAKES 96 TORTILLA CHIPS

12 (6-inch) round corn tortillas (white or yellow)

2 tablespoons extra virgin olive oil

1 teaspoon salt

Preheat oven to 400 degrees.

Brush both sides of the tortilla with oil. Stack 6 of them together and, using kitchen shears or scissors, cut the stack into 8 triangles, for a total of 48 chips. Repeat with the final 6 tortillas. Scatter the chips in a single layer onto a large cookie sheet and sprinkle them evenly with salt. Bake 10 minutes, then flip them using a wide spatula and bake for another 8 to 10 minutes until crispy and golden brown.

Serve with Tricky Taco Soup, page 172, Bravo Nacho Cheese Dip, page 180, or No Doc Guac, page 183.

Cheesy Chip Variation

Nutrition Highlights: Whole grains and calcium • Rich in vitamins E and B1 (thiamin), folate, calcium, potassium, and fiber (added benefit: no gluten)

1 cup low-fat grated cheddar cheese

Follow exact directions and ingredients for Crunchy Corn Chips, but sprinkle the grated cheese evenly over the chips during the last 10 minutes of cooking time.

Cinnamon-Sugar Chip Variation

1 teaspoon sugar

½ teaspoon cinnamon

Mix sugar and cinnamon in a small bowl or plastic bag. Following directions and ingredients for Crunchy Corn Chips, simply substitute the sugar-cinnamon mix for salt and sprinkle evenly on chips before baking.

The American Heart Association recommends limiting the use of harmful trans fats to less than 1 percent of total calories for Americans age 2 and older. It is not enough to simply reduce fat in the diet; it is important to consider the type of fat.

Bravo Nacho Cheese Dip

Nutrition Highlights: Calcium, protein, and vegetables · Rich in vitamins A, C, and K, manganese, fiber, calcium, and tryptophan

Melted American cheese was as close as I could come in texture to the silky smooth feeling of the nacho cheese dips at the movies or ball games. Other cheeses like cheddar melted into a stringy mess. The carrots and yams actually help the texture, adding a hint of sweetness to this dip. This is all in addition to their fantastic nutrition-boosting properties.

MAKES ABOUT 1 CUP

4 ounces (or 6 slices) American cheese

¼ cup milk

¼ cup Orange Puree (See Make-Ahead Recipe #2)

Combine cheese, milk, and Orange Puree in a microwave-safe bowl. Cover the top of the bowl with a wet paper towel and microwave on high for 2 to 3 minutes, stopping to check and stir every 30 seconds until fully melted. Alternatively, you can cook mixture over a double boiler or in a metal bowl over a pot of boiling water.

This dip thickens as it cools, so if there is a delay in serving it, simply put it back in the microwave for another 30 seconds first.

Serve with Crunchy Corn Chips on page 178, pretzel sticks, or over broccoli or other veggies.

Quick Fix for Ranch Dressing

Nutrition Highlights: Calcium and probiotics · Rich in iodine, probiotics, calcium, and protein

On the occasion that I've seen kids eat raw carrot sticks, it's usually just as a carrier for ranch dressing. I'm not sure what it is that kids love about it so much, but its popularity is nearly universal. Unfortunately, it's loaded with saturated fat and MSG (monosodium glutamate). The best-tasting bottled dressing I've found without MSG is Newman's Own Ranch Dressing. By mixing in some plain yogurt, you can increase the volume and cut the fat, as well as adding some "friendly live bacteria." Gradually increase the amount of yogurt over time until the ratio is almost even.

3 tablespoons bottled ranch dressing

1 to 2 tablespoons low-fat plain yogurt

Mix well. Serve as dip or dressing.

Cinnamon Sugar Rattle Snacks

Nutrition Highlights: Beans · Rich in vitamins B6 and C, manganese, folate, iron, fiber, and protein

Roasted crunchy chickpeas were made popular by the low-carb diets, and borrowing from that philosophy, I've added kid-favorite sugar and cinnamon to entice them to crunch on this high-fiber, high-protein snack.

---

2 teaspoons sugar

1 teaspoon cinnamon

¼ teaspoon salt

1 15-ounce can chickpeas,
   drained and rinsed

Preheat oven to 350 degrees.

Combine sugar, cinnamon, and salt in a bowl and add chickpeas. Toss until well coated. Spread on an ungreased cookie sheet, and bake for 55 to 60 minutes, shaking the sheet and mixing occasionally until the chickpeas are crisp and "rattle" on the pan.

No Doc Guac

Nutrition Highlights: Fruit and vegetables · Rich in vitamins A, C, and K, iron, potassium, folate, magnesium, manganese, calcium, and fiber

Mexican night at our house is not just fun, it also provides one of our healthiest meals. Avocado is one of the most nutrient-dense fruits (yes, it's a fruit!) on earth, and provides an excellent hiding place for the pureed broccoli, spinach, and peas in the Green Puree. I've omitted the chopped raw onion and spicy jalapeños that are found in most guacamole recipes, but feel free to add them if your family won't object.

MAKES ABOUT 4 SMALL SERVINGS

1 ripe avocado

½ lime, freshly squeezed

½ teaspoon salt

2 to 4 tablespoons Green Puree (See Make-Ahead Recipe #3)

Halve the avocado lengthwise, remove the pit, and scoop out the flesh. In a small bowl, combine the avocado with the lime juice, salt, and Green Puree and blend well with a fork.

Goes well with Crunchy Corn Chips, page 178, or Total Tacos, page 210.

No Sin Potato Skins

Nutrition Highlights: Vegetables, calcium · Rich in vitamins B6, C, manganese, folate, tryptophan, potassium, calcium and fiber

Potato skins, the ultimate indulgence. Usually deep fried and drenched in butter, melted cheese, bacon and high fat sour cream, they might as well be called potato sins! Some simple tweaking converts these skins into a delivery system for some nutrient-packed veggies with a bit of heart-healthy olive oil. Note: Potato skins can be scooped out and spread with puree and cheese (but not baked) one day ahead and chilled, loosely covered with foil.

MAKES 4 SERVINGS

2 large russet potatoes, scrubbed

¼ cup White Puree (see Make-Ahead Recipe #4)

¼ cup shredded low fat Cheddar or Colby cheese

2 tablespoons butter, melted

Salt

Optional garnishes: bacon bits, low fat sour cream

Preheat oven to 450 degrees and spray a baking sheet with oil.

Prick potatoes several times with a fork and place them directly on oven rack. Bake for 50 to 60 minutes until tender. Remove potatoes from the oven and set aside until cool enough to handle. Turn oven to high broil.

Cut potatoes in half lengthwise and carefully scoop out the flesh leaving about one-quarter inch-thick shells (save the leftover flesh in the refrigerator for up to 3 days for another use, such as mashed potatoes.

Place shells, skin side down, on the prepared baking sheet and brush both sides of the potatoes with melted butter. Sprinkle with a pinch of salt. With the back of a spoon, spread about one tablespoon of White Puree on the inside of each potato skin, covering the sides and bottom evenly. Top with about 2 tablespoons of cheese, and then broil, about 6 inches from the heat, for 8 to 10 minutes until bubbly brown. Serve immediately.

Serve with a dollop of low fat sour cream (or plain yogurt) and fresh bacon bits, if kids like.

White Bean Puree Variation

Follow instructions for No Sin Potato Skins, but replace the White Puree with the same amount of White Bean Puree (see Make-Ahead Recipe #9).

Sneaky Tip:

Teach kids the difference between whole foods grown in nature and those synthetically manufactured in a factory. Play the "where did this come from?" game at the table, identifying which foods are manmade and which grew naturally.

Cheesy Animal Crackers

Nutrition Highlights: whole grains, calcium, and protein · Rich in vitamins B and E, iron, potassium, folic acid, manganese, folate, tryptophan, calcium, protein, and fiber

This recipe combines kids' favorite animal-shaped crackers with the cheesy taste most of them love. But unlike many recipes for homemade cheese crackers that start with a stick of butter and tons of cheese, these crispy gems boast hidden pureed chickpeas, a little olive oil, and lots of whole grains. They make a nutritious mini-meal or a great complement to soups, and they conveniently keep for weeks at room temperature in an airtight container or for six months in the freezer. The kids chose a mini-duck cookie cutter and helped cut the shapes; it's always more likely that they'll eat what they themselves helped prepare. These crackers are one of the easiest ways I have found to sneak the missing fiber back into their diets.

MAKES APPROXIMATELY 48 SMALL CRACKERS

⅓ cup Chickpea Puree (see Make-Ahead Recipe #10)

½ cup grated low-fat cheddar cheese

2 tablespoons grated Parmesan cheese

2 tablespoons extra virgin olive oil

¼ teaspoon salt

¼ teaspoon onion powder

¼ teaspoon paprika

⅓ cup Flour Blend (See Make-Ahead Recipe #13)

Small (about 1 to 2 inch) animal-shaped cookie cutters

Preheat oven to 375 degrees and line a baking sheet with parchment paper (or spray with oil).

In a mixing bowl, combine Chickpea Puree with cheeses, oil, salt, onion powder, and paprika. Add Flour Blend and mix until well blended. Remove the mixture from the bowl and shape into a flattened ball using your hands. If dough is too crumbly, add 1 teaspoon of water at a time, until it holds together.

Wrap in parchment or plastic and chill for at least 30 minutes (or up to 1 day).

Let the dough soften slightly at room temperature and then roll it out onto a lightly floured surface with a lightly floured rolling pin until about $\frac{1}{16}$ inch thin. Cut out fun shapes using cookie cutters. (If you want the kids to help, this is the fun part. Just don't mention the chickpeas!) Place on prepared cookie sheets and lightly spray the top sides of the crackers with oil.

Bake until golden brown on the edges, about 10 to 12 minutes, peeking in the oven occasionally to make sure they're not burning. Transfer crackers to a rack to cool.

Goes well with Creative Cream of Tomato Soup, page 169, or Creamy Chicken Noodle Soup, page 170.

Label alert! At all costs, avoid the top 3 offenders in kids' packaged foods: partially hydrogenated oil (trans fats), high fructose corn syrup (HFCS), and monosodium glutamate (MSG).

Trans fats are known to increase LDL or "bad" cholesterol, while lowering levels of HDL or "good" cholesterol, and can cause clogging of the arteries, increasing the risk of heart disease.

Recent studies suggest that because of the way HFCS is metabolized, it may be a contributor to the growing obesity epidemic and possibly promote diabetes.

MSG, an additive that enhances the flavor of food, can cause headaches, heart palpitations, lightheadedness, and other reactions in MSG-sensitive individuals.

Frozen Applesauce

Nutrition Highlights: Fruit and fiber · Rich in vitamins C, E, and K, manganese, antioxidants, and fiber

Applesauce is a staple for most children, but it can be a bit boring. One day I decided to toss one of the little plastic tubs in the freezer to make a special treat. It came out like an Italian ice and the kids were thrilled with this novelty. It also makes a great place to hide some real fruit purees, which naturally flavor the applesauce. Pouring this mixture into a popsicle mold gives applesauce a whole new shape and makes it a special treat (especially when it means the kids are allowed to have popsicles for breakfast). You can add some terrific extra nutrients to the applesauce.

EACH VARIATION MAKES 3 TO 4 SERVINGS

Blueberry Apple:

1 cup applesauce

½ cup Blueberry Juice (See Make-Ahead Recipe #6)

Cherry Apple:

1 cup applesauce

½ cup Cherry Juice (See Make-Ahead Recipe #7)

Strawberry Apple:

1 cup applesauce

½ cup Strawberry Juice (See Make-Ahead Recipe #8)

In a mixing bowl, combine applesauce and fresh fruit juice. Mix well until liquid is fully incorporated. Pour fruit mixture into popsicle molds or mini plastic containers with lids and freeze until firm. Remove from freezer and let soften for a few minutes before serving.

If you don't have popsicle molds on hand, you can use paper cups. Simply fill cups with mixture and cover them with a piece of aluminum foil. Make a slit in the foil over the center of each cup and insert a wooden stick. Freeze popsicles until firm. Run warm water on the outside of cup to loosen each popsicle from the sides.

Grab 'n' Go Crispy Granola Bars

Nutrition Highlights: Calcium, whole grains and nuts (optional) · Rich in vitamins B2 (riboflavin), D and E, iron, potassium, manganese, selenium, folic acid, tryptophan, calcium, protein, and fiber

*My first few batches of traditional homemade granola bars, with all those visible oats, seeds, and dried fruit definitely did not fly among our taste testers. They looked and tasted far too **healthy**—a definite no-no for a successful sneaky chef! I decided to replace the seeds with blander-tasting almonds and replace half of the oats with the fun texture of a crispy brown rice cereal. Grinding the oats and almonds was critical to the kid appeal, so I didn't mind the extra few seconds of effort. The result ended up being a cross between a granola bar and a Rice Krispies treat.*

These bars are far healthier than kids' breakfast cereals, delivering a good boost of whole grains and fiber, as well as calcium from the powdered milk. I put some in little plastic bags frozen individually to keep them from going stale, and toss them in lunch boxes or for a snack on the run.

⅔ cup rolled oats, ground in a food processor to about ½ cup

½ cup blanched, slivered almonds, ground in a food processor to about ⅓ cup (omit if allergic, and add another ⅓ cup of ground oats instead)

¼ cup wheat germ

1 cup crispy brown rice cereal (or Rice Krispies)

1 cup nonfat dry milk

½ teaspoon cinnamon

½ teaspoon salt

½ cup canola oil

½ cup honey

1 teaspoon pure vanilla extract

¼ cup chocolate chips (optional)

Optional extra boost:

¼ cup raisins or dried blueberries

Preheat oven to 300 degrees. Line a 9-inch square or 13-by-9 inch baking pan completely with foil and butter the foil (or spray with oil).

In a medium bowl, combine oats, almonds (if using), wheat germ, cereal, dry milk, cinnamon, and salt. Mix in the canola oil, honey, vanilla extract, and chocolate chips (and/or dried fruit, optional). Mix well, then pour into the prepared baking pan. Press down with palm of hand, evenly distributing the mixture into the corners of the dish and bake for 15 to 18 minutes. Check occasionally to prevent burning.

Remove from the oven and using the foil to help you, lift the giant bar out of pan. Place on a flat surface and while still warm, cut into small bars.

Store in an airtight container for up to a week, or freeze in plastic bags.

Sneaky Tip:

Measure the oil first, then the honey. That way the honey won't stick and will slide right out of the measuring cup.

Quick Fixes for Applesauce

Nutrition Highlights: fruit

Most berry-flavored applesauce uses artificial colors and flavors. The following additions do notice-ably change the color and taste of the applesauce, but there is no objectionable fruit pulp, and if your kids like flavored applesauce, this is a great upgrade.

Try to choose applesauce that doesn't have artificial colors or flavors, high fructose corn syrup, or any other added sweeteners. Mix one of the following boosters into 1 cup of applesauce. Stir until well combined. Serve in the original little plastic tubs for real authenticity.

---

* 2 to 4 tablespoons Blueberry Juice

(see Make-Ahead Recipe #6)

Rich in vitamins C and E, manganese, antioxidants, and fiber

* 2 to 4 tablespoons Cherry Juice

(See Make-Ahead Recipe #7)

Rich in vitamins A and C, potassium, antioxidants, and fiber

* 2 to 4 tablespoons Strawberry Juice

(See Make-Ahead Recipe #8)

Rich in vitamins C, and K, manganese, antioxidants, and fiber

* 2 to 4 tablespoons pomegranate juice

Rich in vitamins A, C, and E, iron, antioxidants, and fiber

> **Label alert! Even if the front of a package claims "no trans fats," flip it over and read the ingredients, looking for partially hydrogenated oils. If it's listed, it's in there, and every little bit adds up.**

DINNER

Triple-Stuffed Potatoes

Nutrition Highlights: Vegetables and calcium · Rich in vitamins C and B6, manganese, calcium, and protein

I grew up on this warm comfort food. They're essentially mashed potatoes stuffed back into a crispy potato skin boat, blanketed by bubbly melted cheese that deliciously hides the extra nutrients beneath. You can gradually work up to the larger amounts of sneaky puree.

MAKES 6 STUFFED HALVES

3 large russet potatoes, scrubbed

¼ to ½ cup White Puree (see Make-Ahead Recipe #4)

¾ cup grated low-fat cheddar cheese, divided

2 tablespoons butter

2 tablespoons low-fat sour cream

½ teaspoon salt

Optional extra boost: mix in ½ cup chopped broccoli or peas

Preheat oven to 450 degrees.

Prick potatoes several times with a fork and place them directly on oven rack. Bake for 50 to 60 minutes until tender. Remove potatoes from the oven and set aside until cool enough to handle. Turn oven to high broil.

Cut potatoes in half lengthwise and carefully scoop out the flesh into a mixing bowl, leaving some potato in the skin to keep shells intact. Mash potatoes lightly with a fork, adding the White Puree, ½ cup of the cheddar cheese, butter, sour cream and salt. Refill the shells with the potato mixture, mounding slightly. Divide the remaining ¼ cup of cheddar among the potatoes and top each potato half with about 1 tablespoon of the grated cheddar. Place on a cookie sheet and broil, about 6 inches from the heat, for 8 to 10 minutes until bubbly brown. Serve immediately.

White Bean Puree Variation

Follow instructions for Triple-Stuffed Potatoes, but replace the White Puree with the same amount of White Bean Puree (see Make-Ahead Recipe #9).

Crunchy Chicken Tenders

Nutrition Highlights: Whole grains, protein, vegetables, and nuts (optional) · Rich in vitamins E, A, K, B3 (niacin), and C, potassium, tryptophan, protein, and fiber

Chicken fingers are consistently found among the top three choices on every kid's menu and fast-food chain in the nation. They are usually deep fried and full of artery-clogging trans fats. With that in mind, I set out to capitalize on the popularity of this finger food, but to transform it from a fast food into a superfood.

The breading technique is standard—the ingredients are anything but. Using the classic "dry/wet/dry" technique, I upgraded the flour to whole grain, then added pureed carrots and sweet potatoes to the egg batter, then enhanced the final breading with wheat germ and almonds (omit if allergic). The pureed vegetables add a hint of sweetness to the chicken, while hiding beautifully under a blanket of crunchy breading. Each time you make this recipe, you can gradually increase the amount of the Orange Puree used in the batter. They may not be able to see the veggies under the crunchy breading, but their little bodies know the nutrients are there and they thank you for the extra effort!

You can pan fry these in a little heart-healthy olive oil or oven bake them if you are short on time in the kitchen.

An Emory University study asked twenty-three children to go organic, and after only three days, the kids' bodies no longer showed traces of two common pesticides: malathion and chlorpyrifos. Once the kids went back to their usual diet, the chemicals returned.

1 pound boneless, skinless chicken tenders
(or boneless, skinless chicken breasts,
cut into strips)

½ teaspoon salt

½ cup flour, preferably whole wheat

2 large eggs

¼ to ½ cup Orange Puree (see Make-Ahead
Recipe #2)

2 cups Better Breading (see Make-Ahead
Recipe #12)

½ cup grated Parmesan cheese

Olive oil for pan frying

Season chicken tenders with salt. Place flour in a shallow dish or on a plate. Beat eggs with Orange Puree in shallow bowl and place next to the flour. In a third shallow dish or on a paper plate, combine the Better Breading with the Parmesan cheese.

Dredge each piece of chicken in the flour, shaking off excess, then the egg mixture, and then the Better Breading mixture. Press the breading evenly onto both sides of the chicken. Put on wax or parchment paper and store in the refrigerator for cooking tomorrow or proceed to cook immediately.

Pan-fry method:

Heat 2 tablespoons of oil in a large skillet over moderately high heat until hot but not smoking. Add a few strips at a time, pan frying on one side until the crumbs look golden, about 2 to 3 minutes. Watch for burning, and turn down heat if necessary. With tongs, turn the pieces over and lightly brown the second side until golden, about 3 minutes. Reduce the heat to low and continue heating chicken until cooked through, about another 10 minutes. Blot cooked tenders on paper towels to remove excess oil.

Oven-bake method (not as brown and crisp, but quicker):

Preheat oven to 400 degrees.

Place breaded tenders on a lightly sprayed cookie sheet and bake for 10 to 12 minutes. Turn chicken tenders over once with tongs, then return to oven for another 10 to 12 minutes until cooked through.

Maxed Out Meatloaf

Nutrition Highlights: Whole grains, protein, and vegetables · Rich in vitamins A, C, and K, folate, manganese, iron, tryptophan, selenium, protein, and fiber

A lot more refined than our moms' "mystery meatloaf," this enhanced version sneaks in a healthy dose of peas, broccoli, and spinach, as well as whole grains from oats and wheat germ. Red from the ketchup helps mask the green color and taste, and taking the extra minute to puree the oats in the food processor ensures that nothing will ignite the kids' "ick" factor. I also find that it's way easier to throw big chunks of onion in the food processor for a minute, than it is to finely mince them by hand (not to mention that it keeps you from crying).

MAKES 6 TO 8 SERVINGS

¼ cup Green Puree (See Make-Ahead Recipe #3)

2 tablespoons tomato paste

4 tablespoons ketchup, divided

1 large egg, beaten

½ medium onion (about ½ cup), finely minced or pureed in a food processor

1 teaspoon Worcestershire sauce

½ cup rolled oats, ground in a food processor

⅓ cup wheat germ, unsweetened

1 teaspoon salt

1 pound lean ground beef or turkey

Cooking spray for baking sheet

Preheat oven to 350 degrees and spray a baking sheet with oil.

In a large bowl, combine the Green Puree and tomato paste, mixing well (with the back of a fork) until the green color turns brownish. Mix in 2 tablespoons of ketchup, egg, onion, Worcestershire, oats, wheat germ, and salt. Add the ground meat to this mixture and mix with your hands until well combined, then shape it into a single rectangular loaf, or 4 mini-loaves, on the prepared baking sheet. Glaze the top and sides of the loaf or loaves with the remaining ketchup, adding a little more if needed to cover the top and sides of the loaf.

Bake for 50 to 55 minutes, until the internal temperature is 160 degrees.

Orange Puree Variation

Follow exact instructions above for Maxed Out Meatloaf, but replace the Green Puree with the same amount of Orange Puree (See Make-Ahead Recipe #2).

Sneaky Tip:

Kids still won't eat it? No problem! Here are three more ways to hide it:

* **Serve cold meatloaf in a sandwich.**
* **Layer meatloaf with cheese and sauce in Gotta Lotta Lasagna, page 204.**
* **Wrap little pieces of meatloaf in wonton wrappers for Undercover Crispy Ravioli, page 203.**

Magic Meatballs

Nutrition Highlights: Whole grains, protein, and vegetables · Rich in vitamins A, K, B12, C, and E, tryptophan, manganese, folate, zinc, protein, iron, and fiber

There's no mystery about the health benefits of these perfectly "normal" looking and tasting meatballs. Yet unlike those at the Italian restaurant, our meatballs are loaded with whole grains and greens. Thanks to a little help from a preschool color wheel, I found that the green disappears into the color of meaty brown when mixed well with the tomato paste. My kids love to eat these off toothpicks or smothered in red sauce on top of their favorite spaghetti. The extras save well for months in the freezer packed in a sealed plastic bag. You can gradually work up to larger amounts of sneaky puree.

MAKES ABOUT 42 SMALL MEATBALLS

6 to 8 tablespoons Green Puree
   (See Make-Ahead Recipe #3)

2 tablespoons tomato paste

1 teaspoon salt

¼ cup wheat germ, unsweetened

1 large egg, beaten

1 pound lean ground beef or turkey

½ cup extra virgin olive oil, for browning
   meatballs

Sneaky Tip:

One-bite mini-meatballs work better than larger ones for hiding purees.

In a large bowl, combine the Green Puree and tomato paste, mixing well (with the back of a fork) until the green color turns brownish. Mix in salt, wheat germ, and egg, and finally add the ground meat and mix with hands until well combined. Using damp hands, pinch off about 2 teaspoons of meat and gently shape mixture into mini meatballs.

(Below are 2 ways to cook the meatballs, depending on how much time you have. You will definitely get out of the kitchen quicker with the oven-baked method, and the result is nearly as good as the pan frying.)

Brown-in-pan method

Heat 2 tablespoons of oil in a large (10 inch or 12 inch) nonstick skillet over moderately high heat, until hot but not smoking. Add meatballs in four batches to avoid overcrowding the pan. Allow to brown on all sides for about 5 minutes, turning occasionally with the help of 2 teaspoons. Reduce heat to low and cook through for another 10 minutes. Transfer to a plate and add more oil as needed for the next batch. Serve with toothpicks as "cocktail" meatballs, dropped in almost any soup, or smothered in Easy Homemade Pasta Sauce, page ___, over spaghetti.

Oven-baked method

Preheat oven to 350 degrees. Brush a large cookie sheet with 2 tablespoons of oil, gently place meatballs on sheet, and bake for 10 minutes. Using a spatula to loosen, turn the meatballs over to brown on the other side, then return to oven for another 10 minutes. Serve with toothpicks as "cocktail" meatballs, dropped in almost any soup, or smothered in Easy Homemade Pasta Sauce over spaghetti.

Sneaky Tip:

A great use for leftover meatballs is Undercover Crispy Ravioli (next page).

"Saucy" Meat Sauce

Nutrition Highlights: protein, vegetables, and beans · Rich in vitamins E, C, A, B12, and K, folate, manganese, iron, potassium, and protein

This fairly traditional meat sauce provides an excellent hiding place for all kinds of healthy additions. Start with the recipe below, but feel free to keep adding other sneaky purees (like White Puree) until it gets too obvious!

MAKES 6 TO 8 SERVINGS

2 tablespoons extra virgin olive oil

1 medium onion, pureed

1 pound lean ground beef or turkey

1 clove garlic, finely minced (or ⅛ teaspoon garlic powder)

½ teaspoon salt

Freshly ground pepper to taste

¼ cup plus 2 tablespoons Orange Puree (See Make-Ahead Recipe #2)

¼ cup White Bean Puree (See Make-Ahead Recipe #9)

1 6-ounce can plus 2 tablespoons tomato paste

1 28-ounce can plum tomatoes, pureed with their juice

2 tablespoons grated Parmesan cheese

Heat oil over medium heat in a deep skillet or earthenware pot. Cook the onions until they are slightly translucent, and then add the beef, stirring to break it up, cooking about 5 minutes until beef is no longer red. Then add the garlic, salt, and a few grinds of pepper. Add the Orange Puree, White Bean Puree, tomato paste, pureed tomatoes, and Parmesan cheese. Reduce heat to low and simmer at least 30 minutes. Serve with any shape pasta, added to the pot of sauce and tossed to coat every piece well.

Double meat sauce recipe and use the extra helping for Gotta Lotta Lasagna, page 204, or freeze and use within three months.

Undercover Crispy Ravioli

Here's a fun way to turn those pesky leftovers (or the dinner your kids wouldn't eat) into a crispy hand-held treat. You're simply going undercover here by wrapping small pieces of leftover meatballs, meatloaf, burgers, or taco meat inside wonton wrappers and browning the wonton in a skillet to seal it tight and make it crispy. They're finger food, which makes it all the more likely that kids will love them.

You can prepare these ravioli with the leftovers and refrigerate for a day or two, then pan fry when you're ready to serve them.

Possible ingredients — use any of the following left-overs:

Maxed Out Meatloaf, page 198

Magic Meatballs, page 200

Total Tacos, page 210

Bonus Burgers, page 224

Wonton wrappers

Olive oil for browning

Lay out several wonton wrappers on the counter. Fill a small bowl with water and place it near you. Dip your fingertips in the water and use them to brush all of the edges of each wrapper. Place a bite-sized piece of the cooked meat (about 1½ teaspoons) in the center of each wrapper. Bring two corners of the wrapper together, forming an *imperfect* triangle. Press the wet edges together to seal.

Add 2 tablespoons of oil to a large skillet and heat over medium-high heat. Turn down to medium if oil starts to smoke. Pan fry about 6 wontons at a time, for 30 seconds to 1 minute, until golden brown. Using tongs, turn the wontons over to brown the other side. Place cooked wontons on a plate lined with paper towels to blot the excess oil. Serve warm as finger food.

Gotta Lotta Lasagna

Nutrition Highlights: Protein, calcium, fiber, and vegetables · Rich in vitamins A, C and K, folate, fiber, manganese, lycopene, tryptophan, and calcium

Ahh, lasagna. The ultimate party food. Only with this sneaky recipe, you can enjoy the party without as much guilt. By using nutrient-rich low-fat tofu (which looks exactly like ricotta when mashed well or pureed), we were able to cut out half of the cheese. We also cut out more than half of the traditional amount of mozzarella from the inner layers (where no one would miss it), yet maintained a rich and bubbly cheese-covered top of the lasagna.

Lasagna presents the ultimate hiding place for all kinds of things (that old tire in the garage?), so feel free to add even more healthy purees to your sauce (for example, White Bean Puree works well here, too).

*The assembly is a bit time consuming, but I found it oddly meditative and it was well worth the effort. This is a great dish to serve for birthday parties or when you're having people over for dinner. Gotta Lotta can be prepared ahead, **without baking**, and refrigerated for a day. Or freeze it in plastic wrap with foil over it for up to three months.*

MAKES 9 TO 12 SERVINGS

1 cup low-fat ricotta cheese

1 cup (half of a 14-ounce block) firm tofu, mashed well or pureed in a food processor

½ teaspoon salt

1 cup White Puree (see Make-Ahead Recipe #4)

3½ cups store-bought tomato sauce or Easy Homemade Pasta Sauce, page 208

12 pieces oven-ready, no-boil lasagna noodles (whole wheat preferred)

2½ cups part-skim shredded mozzarella cheese

¼ cup grated Parmesan cheese

If you are using Easy Homemade Pasta Sauce, page 208, add 4½ cups of that sauce and omit the additional White Puree in this recipe.

Preheat oven to 350 degrees and spray a 13-by-9 glass baking dish with oil.

In a medium bowl, mix the ricotta with the mashed (or pureed) tofu and salt. In another bowl, mix the White Puree into the tomato sauce (omit this step if using Easy Homemade Pasta Sauce that already has the purees mixed in).

To assemble the lasagna:

Spread ¾ cup of sauce on the bottom of the prepared baking dish.

Place 3 pieces of uncooked pasta on top of the sauce, side by side (but not overlapping).

Spread ⅔ cup of the ricotta/tofu mixture evenly over the pasta.

Spread ¾ cup of tomato sauce evenly over the ricotta, covering the pasta completely.

Sprinkle ½ cup of mozzarella cheese over the top of the sauce.

This is the first layer. Now repeat steps 2 through 5 *two* more times. Finally, top with the remaining 3 pasta pieces and spread the remaining tomato sauce completely over the top of the pasta, then sprinkle with the remaining mozzarella cheese and all of the Parmesan cheese.

Cover lasagna with foil sprayed with oil. Bake 30 minutes. Uncover. Bake another 15 to 20 minutes or until the top is lightly browned. Let stand a few minutes before cutting.

A note about soy: although I don't recommend highly processed soy products (such as isolated soy protein in protein bars), I feel a little tofu or whole soybeans are fine for children in moderation.

No Harm Chicken Parm

Nutrition Highlights: whole grains, nuts, protein, and vegetables · Rich in vitamins A, B complex, C and K, tryptophan, selenium, lycopene, iron, folate, magnesium, manganese, calcium, protein, and fiber

This is essentially a large, thin chicken nugget covered in sauce and cheese, which together provide ample opportunity to sneak in at least four vegetables, none of which is visible to the eye or detectable by the taste buds. As if that weren't enough, to make the dish even healthier, whole-grain breading replaces traditional bread crumbs made from nutritionally empty white bread. This recipe converts a decadent dish into a nutritional superstar and a favorite for the kid in all of us.

MAKES 4 TO 6 SERVINGS

4 boneless, skinless chicken breast halves, about 1 pound

½ teaspoon salt

½ cup whole wheat flour

2 large eggs

¼ to ½ cup Green Puree (see Make-Ahead Recipe #3)

1½ cups Better Breading (see Make-Ahead Recipe #12)

Olive oil for pan frying

1½ cups grated part-skim mozzarella

1 cup store-bought tomato sauce (or Easy Homemade Pasta Sauce, page 208)

½ cup grated Parmesan

Preheat oven to 375 degrees.

Place each chicken half between two sheets of plastic wrap and pound until very thin with a mallet or rolling pin. Season chicken with salt. Place flour in a shallow dish or on a plate. Beat eggs with Green Puree in another shallow bowl and place it next to the flour. Put the Better Breading in a third shallow dish or on a plate.

Dredge each piece of chicken in the flour and shake off excess, then dip in the egg mixture, and then in the Better Breading mixture. Press the breading evenly onto both sides of the chicken. Lay the pieces on waxed or parchment paper and store in the refrigerator for cooking the next day or proceed to cook immediately.

Heat 2 tablespoons oil in a large non-stick skillet over moderately high heat until hot but not smoking. Add two pieces of chicken at a time, pan frying on one side until the crumbs look golden, about 2 to 3 minutes. Watch for burning and turn down heat if necessary. With tongs, turn the pieces over and lightly brown the second side until golden, about 3 minutes. Place pan-fried chicken pieces on a large baking sheet, sprayed with cooking oil.

Top each chicken breast with about ¼ cup of tomato sauce and cover sauce with mozzarella and a sprinkling of Parmesan. Bake 15 to 20 minutes or until cheese is lightly browned and bubbly.

Serve with whole wheat spaghetti and tomato sauce.

Sneaky Tip:

Never ask open-ended questions like "What do you want for dinner?" Instead, give limited choices such as, "Would you prefer spaghetti or mac 'n' cheese for dinner?"

Easy Homemade Pasta Sauce

Nutrition Highlights: Vegetables · Rich in vitamins A, C and K, lycopene, manganese, folate, and fiber

MAKES ABOUT 4 CUPS SAUCE

¼ cup extra virgin olive oil

1 onion, finely minced or
   pureed

1 clove garlic, finely minced

¼ cup Orange Puree (See
   Make-Ahead Recipe #2)

¼ cup White Puree (See
   Make-Ahead Recipe #4)

1 can, about 28 ounces,
   whole peeled tomatoes
   with liquid

1 6-ounce can tomato paste

½ teaspoon salt

Freshly ground pepper

Place oil in a deep saucepan over medium heat. Cook the onions and garlic until they are slightly translucent but not brown, stirring occasionally. Mix in the Orange and White Purees, tomatoes, and tomato paste and bring to a boil. Lower the heat and simmer for 15 to 20 minutes until sauce thickens. Transfer sauce to a blender and puree in batches, or use a handheld blender inserted directly in the pot to puree sauce.

Stir in salt and a few grinds of pepper, to taste. Use immediately or store covered in the refrigerator for up to 1 week, or freeze for up to 6 months.

Pink Sauce Variation

Nutrition Highlights: Calcium and vegetables

Add one 5-ounce can (about ¾ cup) evaporated low-fat milk to above recipe for Easy Homemade Pasta Sauce, mixing until well blended and continue simmering to thicken the sauce. Puree sauce as instructed above.

Sneaky Tip:

To avoid scalding your hands when using a blender with hot liquids, let the liquid cool for a few minutes, then fill the blender no more than halfway and cover the closed top with a kitchen towel. Pulse a few times before letting the blender run on high speed.

Total Tacos

Nutrition Highlights: Fruit, vegetables, and protein · Rich in vitamins A, B, C, E and K, calcium, magnesium, selenium, manganese, folate, iron, lycopene, tryptophan, protein, and fiber

These tacos are deliberately mild, so they will appeal to a wide variety of palates. If your kids like the taste of packaged taco seasoning or taco sauce, you can simply add it to this recipe. Allowing your children to fill their own taco shells is not only fun for them, but it also makes it more likely that they will eat what they prepared.

MAKES 12 SMALL TACOS

1 tablespoon extra virgin olive oil

1 onion, finely minced or pureed

1 pound lean ground beef or turkey

¼ teaspoon salt

Freshly ground pepper

½ cup Purple Puree (See Make-Ahead Recipe #1)

¾ cup mild salsa*

¼ cup tomato paste

12 hard taco shells

Optional toppings: shredded lettuce, grated low-fat cheddar cheese, chopped fresh tomatoes, low-fat sour cream

Heat oil in a deep skillet over medium heat. Cook the onions until they are slightly translucent and then add the beef (or turkey), stirring to break it up, cooking about 5 minutes until meat is no longer red. Add the salt, a few grinds of pepper, Purple Puree, salsa, and tomato paste and mix well until heated through and the colors blend into a brown mixture, stirring occasionally, about 5 minutes.

Help kids to spoon about ¼ cup filling into each taco shell. Add toppings as desired.

Goes well with No Doc Guac, page 183.

Sneaky Tip:

If salsa is too chunky and you think that might cause kids to object, just puree it in the food processor before mixing it into the taco meat.

Incognito Burritos

Nutrition Highlights: Beans, whole grains, vegetables, and calcium · Rich in fiber, manganese, vitamin C, folate, tryptophan, magnesium, iron, protein, and calcium

If your kids like the simple Taco Bell bean burritos, they should love these. They're as manageable as the thin fast-food burritos, but we've replaced their high-fat refried beans with the canned low-fat variety and also snuck in a good amount of nutrient-rich cauliflower and zucchini. You can prepare these ahead of time, roll them up individually in parchment paper (for that authentic fast-food feeling), and simply reheat for 30 seconds in the microwave when you're ready to serve.

MAKES 4 THIN BURRITOS

½ cup canned low-fat
   refried beans

¼ cup White Puree (See
   Make-Ahead Recipe #4)

4 6-inch flour tortillas
   (whole wheat preferred)

½ cup low-fat shredded
   cheddar cheese

Optional toppings:

   Mexican red sauce,
   salsa, shredded lettuce,
   chopped tomatoes

Spoon refried beans and White Puree into a microwave-safe bowl. Cover the top of the bowl with a wet paper towel and microwave on high for 30 seconds, then mix well. Alternatively, combine refried beans and White Puree in a saucepan and warm through over low heat on stovetop. Place tortillas between moist paper towels and microwave on high for 30 seconds.

To assemble burritos:

Spoon about 2 tablespoons bean mixture onto the bottom third of each tortilla. Top with 1 to 2 tablespoons cheese and any optional toppings. Fold the end of the tortilla closest to you over the filling ingredients and then fold the right end over next and roll up. One end of the burrito is left open and unfolded. Repeat with the next 3 burritos.

Goes well with Crunchy Corn Chips, page 178, and No Doc Guac, page 183.

Sneaky Tip:

To calculate fiber grams per day for kids aged two to twenty: Take the age of the child and add five to find out how many grams of fiber are needed for one day. For example, a nine-year-old child needs fourteen grams of fiber per day (9 + 5 = 14 grams per day).

Power Pizza

Nutrition Highlights: Vegetables, beans, calcium, fiber, and protein · Rich in vitamins A, C, and K, magnesium, iron, lycopene, manganese, folate, tryptophan, fiber, protein, and calcium

With uncooked pizza dough on hand, or just some pocketless pita breads, this pizza is quicker to make than calling out for delivery from the local pizza place. And I'm sure Tony's not sneaking carrots, yams, and beans into his sauce! I mix the healthy purees right into the bottle of store-bought tomato sauce (it looks perfectly normal), then I let the kids do the rest, adding any additional toppings they like. They've never once suspected anything in the sauce, especially under that blanket of bubbly cheese.

You can even prepare this pizza ahead of time without cooking it, and then refrigerate for a day or two. Simply bake when you're ready to eat.

MAKES 1 LARGE PIZZA OR 4 SMALLER PIZZAS

1 store bought pizza dough or 4 "Greek style" pocketless pitas (whole wheat preferred)

¾ cup store-bought tomato sauce* (or 1 cup Easy Homemade Pasta Sauce, pg. 208)

3 tablespoons Orange Puree (See Make-Ahead Recipe #2)

¼ cup White Bean Puree (See Make-Ahead Recipe #9)

1 to 2 cups low-fat shredded mozzarella cheese

Optional extra boost: **sliced mushrooms, onions, sweet peppers, or artichoke hearts**

If using Easy Homemade Pasta Sauce, page 208, add 1 cup of that sauce and omit the additional Orange Puree.

Preheat oven to 400 degrees and preheat a pizza stone, if using one, or spray a baking sheet with oil.

Stretch pizza dough, or roll out with floured rolling pin on floured surface, to form a pie and transfer it to the stone or baking sheet. If using pocketless pitas, place them on the prepared baking sheet. Combine tomato sauce with White Bean and Orange Purees. Mix well. Spread ½ to 1 cup of the sauce mixture across the large pizza dough (use only ¼ cup of sauce for each pita), then top with about 1 cup of mozzarella (use about ½ cup of cheese per pita). Cover and refrigerate at this point, or bake for 15 to 20 minutes until bubbly and lightly browned. Allow to cool a few minutes, then cut into triangles and serve.

Hi-Fi Fish Sticks

Nutrition Highlights: Protein, fiber, and omega-3s · Rich in vitamins B12, C, E, and K, riboflavin, selenium, tryptophan, folate, iron, potassium, manganese, fiber, protein, and omega-3s.

Hi-Fi stands for high fiber and whole grains in this crunchy yet lower fat version of deep-fried fish sticks. The powerful nutrients of the cauliflower and zucchini in the White Puree slip silently under the blanket of breading, but the body knows they're there and thanks you for the extra effort.

MAKES 4 TO 6 SERVINGS

½ cup flour, preferably whole wheat

½ teaspoon salt

2 large eggs

½ cup White Puree (See Make-Ahead Recipe #4)

2 cups Better Breading (See Make-Ahead Recipe #12)

1 pound tilapia or flounder filets, cut into 1-inch wide strips

Olive oil for pan frying

Lemon wedges

Combine flour and salt in a shallow dish or a plate. Beat eggs with White Puree in another shallow bowl and place next to the flour. Put the Better Breading in a third shallow dish or on a plate.

Dredge each piece of fish first in the flour and shake off the excess, then dip in the egg mixture, and then the Better Breading mixture. Press the breading evenly onto both sides of the fish. Lay on waxed or parchment paper and store in the refrigerator for cooking the next day or proceed to cook immediately.

Pan-fry method

Heat 2 tablespoons oil in a large skillet over moderately high heat until hot but not smoking. Add a few fish sticks at a time, pan frying on one side until the crumbs look golden, about 2 to 3 minutes. Watch for burning, and turn down heat if necessary. With a spatula, turn the pieces over and lightly brown the second side until golden, about 3 minutes. Reduce the heat to low and continue heating fish until cooked through, about another 2 to 3 minutes. Blot cooked fish on paper towels to remove excess oil. Serve with lemon wedges.

Oven-bake method (not as brown and crisp, but quicker)

Preheat oven to 400 degrees.

Place breaded fish sticks on a lightly sprayed cookie sheet. Spray the top side of the fish with oil and bake for about 6 minutes. With a spatula, turn fish over once and then return to oven for another 4 to 6 minutes until fish is cooked through and firm to the touch. Serve with lemon wedges.

Goes well with No-Fry Fries, page 220.

Researchers at the University of Sydney have found that children who regularly eat fresh, oily fish have four times lower the risk of developing asthma than do children who rarely eat such fish.

Oven Fried Drumsticks

Nutrition Highlights: Whole grains, vegetables and protein · Rich in vitamins B complex, C and E, iron, potassium, folate, manganese, protein, and fiber

This chicken starts out skinless and then is oven-fried, which eliminates two of the sins of deep-fried chicken. It also delivers a nice dose of fiber and a crispy crunch from the wheat germ and whole grain cereal. If your children don't like the taste of ranch dressing, then feel free to substitute an equal amount of their favorite dressing or plain yogurt.

MAKES 8 DRUMSTICKS

2 cups whole grain cereal
  flakes (such as Wheaties
  or Total)

¼ cup wheat germ,
  unsweetened

½ teaspoon salt

½ cup White Puree (See
  Make-Ahead Recipe #4)

2 tablespoons bottled
  ranch dressing

8 chicken legs, skinless

Preheat oven to 400 degrees.

Using a rolling pin, gently crush the cereal in a sealed plastic bag into coarsely ground crumbs. Alternatively, you can quickly grind the cereal in a food processor. Pour crushed cereal on a plate (or keep some in a plastic bag for future use), and add wheat germ and salt. Mix well.

Pour ranch dressing and White Puree into a large plastic bag. Drop the drumsticks in the plastic bag and coat with the dressing mixture. At this point, you can refrigerate the chicken for as much time as you have, up to a day (this helps add flavor and tenderizes the chicken), or proceed to next step.

Roll each drumstick in the cereal mixture, pressing the crumbs evenly onto the chicken. Set drumsticks onto a baking sheet sprayed with oil. Also spray the top side of the chicken legs evenly with oil. Cook for 45 to 50 minutes, until the chicken is lightly browned and cooked through.

Goes well with Crispy No-Fry Fries, page 220.

A study reported in **Pediatrics 2003** found that children who watch TV at mealtime consume 5 percent fewer fruits and vegetables, and 5 percent more junk food and soda.

Sneaky Tip:

Borrow a pail from the kids' beach toys, line with a cloth napkin or parchment paper, and serve the chicken right inside it.

Crispy No-Fry Fries

Nutrition Highlights: Vegetables and whole grains · Rich in vitamins B complex and C, folate, antioxidants, and fiber

The humble russet potato surprised the health community and took top honors recently with one of the highest disease-fighting antioxidant ratings of all vegetables. That's not to say that we should all run out to eat french fries, which are full of saturated fat. This low-fat version uses a touch of heart-healthy olive oil and a dusting of cornmeal to help mimic the texture of the deep-fried variety that is so often lacking in oven-baked fries. It also adds a bit of extra fiber and whole grain nutrition. Egg whites cut down on the need for a lot of oil and also help the potatoes achieve a nice golden crust.

If you want to scrub and cut the potatoes earlier in the day or even the day before, simply place the wedges in a bowl of water and refrigerate until ready to cook, and then pat dry before proceeding.

MAKES 4 SERVINGS

2 russet potatoes

1 large egg white

1 tablespoon extra-virgin olive oil

½ teaspoon salt

1 tablespoon cornmeal

Preheat oven to 400 degrees.

Cut each potato into 8 wedges or several thin sticks. Toss potatoes in a mixing bowl with the egg white, olive oil, and salt, coating evenly. Then dust the potatoes with cornmeal and spread them in a single layer on a baking sheet sprayed with oil.

Bake 50 to 60 minutes or until golden brown.

Goes well with Hi-Fi Fish Sticks, page 216, Crunchy Chicken Tenders, page 196 or Bonus Burgers, page 224.

Cheese Fry variation

Use the same method as No-Fry Fries, but sprinkle with 1 to 2 tablespoons of grated Parmesan cheese at the same time you dust with the cornmeal.

Sneaky Tip:

Serve these fries in an ice cream parfait (or regular) glass lined with parchment paper sticking out of the top.

Quick Fixes for Store-Bought Tomato Sauce

Each of the nutritional boosters below not only enhances the nutritional profile of your children's favorite bottled pasta sauce, but also helps to cut the acidity of the tomatoes, which may alleviate any upset stomach. Each booster has proven to be undetectable in taste, and any slight change in color can quickly be reversed by adding a little canned tomato paste. Start by adding the least amount recommended of just one of the following nutritional boosters. Add a little more each time you serve this sauce. You can also mix two or more of the boosters below, up to about ½ cup total per 1 cup of store-bought tomato sauce.

**EACH OF THE FOLLOWING QUICK FIXES ARE
FOR 1 CUP OF BOTTLED SAUCE:**

----

* 2 to 4 tablespoons White Bean Puree
  (See Make-Ahead Recipe #9)

Combine White Bean Puree with store-bought sauce, mixing until well blended.

* 2 to 4 tablespoons White Puree
  (See Make-Ahead Recipe #4)

Combine White Puree with store-bought sauce, mixing until well blended. If the sauce becomes too light, simply mix in a tablespoon or so of canned tomato paste to bring the color back to a deeper red.

* 2 to 4 tablespoons Orange Puree
  (See Make-Ahead Recipe #2)

Combine Orange Puree with store-bought sauce, mixing until well blended. If the sauce becomes too light, simply mix in a tablespoon or so of canned tomato paste to bring the color back to a deeper red.

* ¼ cup evaporated milk

Combine evaporated milk with store-bought sauce, mixing until well blended. This makes more of a pink sauce.

Camouflage Joes

Nutrition Highlights: Vegetables and protein · Rich in vitamins A, B12, C and K, iron, folate, zinc, tryptophan, lycopene, manganese, protein, and fiber

Sloppy Joes may be a family favorite from the past, but I'll bet our moms never mixed in cauliflower and zucchini. The familiar taste of ketchup acts as a great decoy for the hidden veggies, and the condensed tomato soup lends an old-fashioned flavor to this heart-warming dish. Feel free to also add some Orange Puree as you experiment with this recipe.

MAKES 6-8 SANDWICHES

1 tablespoon extra-virgin olive oil

1 medium onion, pureed or very
   finely chopped

1 pound lean ground beef or turkey

¼ teaspoon salt

1 can (10¾ ounce) tomato soup,
   condensed

¼ cup ketchup

¼ to ½ cup White Puree (see Make-
   Ahead Recipe #4)

4 to 6 hamburger buns (preferably
   whole wheat)

Heat oil over medium heat in a deep skillet or earthenware pot. Cook the onions until they are slightly translucent, and then add the beef, stirring to break it up, cooking about 5 minutes until beef is no longer red. Add the salt, tomato soup, ketchup, and White Puree. Reduce heat to low and simmer about 5 to 10 minutes, stirring occasionally until the ingredients are well combined. Ladle generously over warm hamburger buns.

Sneaky Tip:

The best way to finely break up ground meat in a pan is to use a rubber-tipped spatula.

Bonus Burgers

Nutrition Highlights: Fruit, vegetables, protein and fiber · Rich in vitamins A, B, C, E and K, calcium, magnesium, selenium, manganese, folate, iron, lycopene, tryptophan, protein, and fiber

In this version of the traditional hamburger, we managed to sneak in a good amount of nutrient-packed pureed blueberries and spinach in the meat. The familiar taste of ketchup helps to override any detectable foreign flavors, and I have yet to find anyone who noticed anything unusual about this burger. If you're adding the optional chickpeas, you will boost the fiber and vitamin content and ensure that all of the saturated fat of the meat is quickly escorted out of the body.

MAKES 8 TO 10 BURGERS

1 large egg

¼ cup Purple Puree (see Make-Ahead Recipe #1)

3 tablespoons ketchup

1 teaspoon salt

¼ cup fresh whole wheat bread crumbs*

1 pound lean ground beef or turkey

8 to 10 American cheese slices (optional)

8 to 10 hamburger buns or English muffins (preferably whole grain)

Pickle slices and ketchup to garnish

Optional extra boost: 2 teaspoons Chickpea Puree (See Make-Ahead Recipe #10)

In a large bowl, mix egg, Purple Puree, ketchup, salt, and bread crumbs. Then add the meat, mixing with hands until well combined. If too sticky, add a few more bread crumbs.

Using damp hands, shape mixture into 8 to 10 patties that are fairly thin. At this point, the burgers may be prepared a day ahead and kept covered in the refrigerator. If you are not freezing for future use, proceed to next steps.

Spray a large skillet or grill pan with non-stick cooking spray and set over moderately high heat until hot but not smoking. Cook the burgers for 3 minutes on each side then flip and add cheese (optional) to melt over patties for another 3 minutes.

Serve on fresh, soft burger buns or English muffins, with ketchup and pickles.

Whole wheat bread crumbs can be found in natural and organic food stores, but you can easily make your own by pulsing whole grain bread in a food processor to achieve fine crumbs. It's that simple. Three slices of bread yield about one cup of fresh crumbs. They keep for months in a sealed bag in the freezer.

A great use for leftover burgers: Undercover Crispy Ravioli, page 203.

Sneaky Tip:

High heat from grilling can react with protein in meat, poultry, and fish to create cancer-causing chemicals HCAs and PAHs. Adding blueberries or cherries to the meat before cooking has been found to significantly reduce this risk.

Sneaky Baked Ziti

Nutrition Highlights: Vegetables, protein, and fiber · Rich in vitamins A, C, and K, lycopene, calcium, tryptophan, manganese, isoflavones, and fiber

Thanks to the versatile blandness of high-fiber, low-fat tofu, and the fact that it bears a striking resemblance to its higher fat twin, mozzarella cheese, we were able to replace at least one-third of the cheese used in traditional baked zitis.

This recipe really passes the sneaky chef challenge, and none of the testers could identify any of the hidden additions. In fact, they proclaimed it the best baked ziti in town! My daughter Emily requested this to be served at her eighth birthday party, and although it was a bit more work than ordering in the usual pizza, the girls gobbled it up.

MAKES 8 TO 10 SERVINGS

1 pound ziti or rigatoni noodles (whole wheat preferred)

1 cup firm tofu, mashed well or pureed in a food processor (½ of a 14 ounce block)

2½ cups store-bought tomato sauce* (or 3½ cups Easy Homemade Pasta Sauce*, pg. 208)

1 cup Orange Puree (see Make-Ahead Recipe #2)

⅓ cup grated parmesan cheese

3 cups shredded part skim mozzarella cheese

If using Easy Homemade Pasta Sauce, use 3½ cups of sauce and omit the additional Orange Puree in this recipe

Preheat oven to 375 degrees and spray a 13-by-9 glass baking dish with oil.

Cook pasta according to package directions until slightly firm. Drain and place in the prepared baking dish. Mix tofu, tomato sauce, and Orange Puree in a bowl. Toss pasta with the sauce mixture and 1 cup of the mozzarella cheese. Top the pasta with a combination of the parmesan and the remaining 2 cups of mozzarella cheese, sprinkling evenly over the top.

Cover ziti with foil. Bake 30 minutes. Uncover. Bake another 10 to 15 minutes or until the top is lightly browned.

White Bean Puree Variation

Follow instructions for Sneaky Baked Ziti, but replace the Orange Puree with the same amount of White Bean Puree (See Make-Ahead Recipe #9). Alternatively, you can add *both* the White Bean and Orange purees in this recipe, for an even healthier dish.

Mystery Mashed Potatoes

Nutrition Highlights: Vegetables, calcium · Rich in vitamins vitamin B6, C, potassium, manganese, folate, calcium and fiber

Comforting, homey, and full of fat, most mashed potato recipes call for a stick of butter and a cup of heavy cream. I used to reserve this dish for major holidays, but with this revamped recipe, we can enjoy these delicious mashed potatoes whenever the urge strikes. You'll hardly miss the heavy cream and butter with the clever use of calcium-rich evaporated skim milk, which is concentrated and has a consistency similar to cream. And the pureed cauliflower and zucchini disappear in the creamy white texture of this dish. For myself, I more than triple the amount of White Puree, since I don't mind the taste of the veggies and I want to cut way back on carbs. But for the family, start at the lower amount of White Puree called for, and gradually increase a little each time you make these, until it gets too noticeable.

MAKES 6 TO 8 SERVINGS

2 pounds Yukon Gold or russet potatoes, peeled and quartered

4 to 8 tablespoons White Puree (see Make-Ahead Recipe #4)

2 tablespoons low fat sour cream

2 tablespoons butter

½ teaspoon salt

¼ cup evaporated skim milk

Place the potatoes in a large pot of cold, salted water and bring to a boil. Lower the heat and simmer covered for 25 to 35 minutes, until the potatoes are completely tender.

Drain potatoes in a colander, and then return to pot along with butter, evaporated milk, White Puree, sour cream and salt. Mash with a potato masher until combined well.

Serve immediately, or keep the mashed potatoes hot on the stovetop in a metal bowl set over simmering water.

White Bean Puree Variation

Follow instructions for Mystery Mashed Potatoes, but replace the White Puree with the same amount of White *Bean* Puree (see Make-Ahead Recipe #9). Alternatively, you can add both the White Bean and White Purees in this recipe, for an even healthier dish.

Cheesy Variation

Cheese acts as an excellent flavor decoy and adds protein and calcium.

Follow instructions for either variation of Mystery Mashed Potatoes, the fold in about ¼ cup shredded low fat cheddar cheese or parmesan cheese to the hot potatoes before serving.

What to do with the leftovers? See the following recipe ...

Leftover Potato Cakes

Nutrition Highlights: Whole grains · Rich in vitamins B6, C, E, iron, potassium, folic acid, manganese, fiber and protein

This recipe can be made from any leftover mashed potatoes (ideally, Mystery Mashed Potatoes, page 228). I came up with this one on the third day after Thanksgiving when our family couldn't bear to eat another serving of mashed potatoes! And by that point, we all needed a little more fiber in our diets, which the wheat germ provides discreetly. My kids like these dipped in applesauce or low fat sour cream.

MAKES 8 SMALL PANCAKES

1 cup leftover mashed
   potatoes

1 to 2 teaspoons whole
   wheat flour

2 to 4 tablespoons olive oil

¼ cup wheat germ,
   unsweetened

2 tablespoons parmesan
   cheese

¼ teaspoon salt

Optional dips: applesauce
   or low fat sour cream

Mix 1 teaspoon of flour into cold, leftover mashed potatoes. If still too wet, add the other teaspoon of flour. Pinch off tablespoon sizes of the mashed potatoes and use your hands to form about 8 balls. Add the oil to a large skillet and heat over medium high heat. Turn down to medium if oil starts to smoke.

Mix the wheat germ with the parmesan cheese and salt on a plate. Roll the balls in the wheat germ mixture, covering completely. Add 4 potato cakes to the hot skillet, flatten gently with a spatula and cook until they have browned on one side, about 1 to 2 minutes. Turns cakes over with a spatula and cook the other side until golden brown, another 1 to 2 minutes. Repeat with next 4 cakes, adding more oil to the pan as needed.

Place cooked potato cakes on a plate lined with paper towels to blot excess oil.

TREATS

Quick Fixes for Jell-O

Most kids love Jell-O, and they can immediately tell you what their favorite flavor is. Although it still has way too much sugar, artificial flavors, and colors to be called a health food, it can become a carrier for healthier antioxidant-rich fruit juices and green tea. Since kids are going to eat it anyway, you can make some simple substitutions that will counter the more troublesome ingredients. For instance, I was excited to learn that green tea might help prevent tooth decay (which would be of assistance here!). And the powerhouse of antioxidants in pomegranate and blueberry juices will counteract just about anything. Each of the substitutions below is for one 3-ounce box of Jell-O. The most adaptable flavors are the red ones—cherry, raspberry or strawberry.

Green Tea and Blueberry Juice

Nutrition Highlights: Fruit and green tea · Rich in vitamins A and C, potassium, folate, flavonoids, and antioxidants

1 cup green tea, boiling, steeped 5 minutes

1 cup cold Blueberry Juice (see Make-Ahead Recipe #6)

Make Jell-O according to directions on box, substituting boiling green tea for boiling water and cold Blueberry Juice for cold water.

Pomegranate, Cherry, or Strawberry Juice

Nutrition Highlights: Fruit · Rich in vitamins B3 (niacin), and C, potassium, folate, and antioxidants

1 cup boiling pomegranate, Cherry or Strawberry Juice (See Make-Ahead Recipe #7 or 8)

1 cup cold pomegranate, Cherry, or Strawberry Juice

Make Jell-O according to directions on box, substituting boiling juice for boiling water and cold juice for cold water.

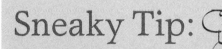

Sneaky Tip:

You can find healthier versions of dessert gelatin at natural food stores, with no artificial colors or flavors.

Jiggly Gelatin Blocks

Nutrition Highlights: Fruit · Rich in vitamins A and C, potassium, folate, flavonoids, and antioxidants

*What a fun way for a child to get almost all of the benefits of the world's healthiest fruit, without having to actually eat the real thing. Even if your child will eat berries or cherries **au naturel**, this is a great way to squeeze a concentrated dose of the good stuff in.*

MAKES ABOUT 100 SMALL BLOCKS

4 cups cold Blueberry, Cherry, or Strawberry Juice (see Make-Ahead Recipe #6, 7, or 8)

4 envelopes Knox unflavored gelatin

2 tablespoons honey or sugar

Pour 1 cup of the Juice into a medium bowl, sprinkle gelatin over it, and let stand for 1 minute. Heat the remaining 3 cups of Juice with the honey or sugar to boiling, stirring occasionally. Add the hot juice to the cold juice and stir until the gelatin completely dissolves, about 5 minutes. Pour into 13-by-9-inch pan.

Refrigerate until firm, about 3 hours. Cut into little squares or use a small cookie cutter to make shapes.

Royal Ice Pops

Nutrition Highlights: Fruit · Rich in vitamins A and C, potassium, folate, flavonoids, and antioxidants

Some kids just won't eat fruit, or they'll only eat one kind. What I have found is that it's usually the appearance or the texture, not the flavor, that turns them away. By making popsicles with juice from real berries, they will reap the benefit of all of the wonderful nutrients with none of the objectionable texture. Even if your kids will eat fruit, these pops are a significant improvement over the artificially flavored and colored ones in the store.

MAKES 4 POPSICLES

1 cup Blueberry, Cherry, or Strawberry Juice (See Make-Ahead Recipe #6, 7, or 8)

4 ice pop molds with sticks

Pour juice into molds, insert stick, and freeze for at least 3 hours.

Unbelievable
Chocolate Chip Cookies

Nutrition Highlights: Whole grains, nuts, and beans · Rich in vitamin E, folate, manganese, selenium, tryptophan, and fiber

*Oats and white beans make a decent chocolate chip cookie, you ask incredulously? **And** I want to throw in wheat germ and whole-wheat flour! Well, tasting is believing. Watch your kids devour these seemingly sinful, yet incredibly nutritious, cookies. This was the hardest recipe to invent. I had to consult with a real baker, my close friend, Karen, who spent many days in the test kitchen with me working out the kinks until we came up with a healthy cookie that didn't taste healthy! First, we were able to cut back on the sugar by **one-third,** resulting in a mere one-half teaspoon of sugar per cookie. Then we added fiber from nutrient-packed wheat germ, whole wheat flour, oats, almonds and white beans, all of which help to slow down the release of sugar and avoid the normal "crash and burn" after kids eat cookies. Karen also convinced me to make them "mini" cookies, so kids could have two for the price of one.*

MAKES ABOUT 50 TWO-BITE COOKIES

1 cup Flour Blend (see Make-Ahead
  Recipe #13)

½ teaspoon baking soda

½ teaspoon salt

¼ cup rolled oats, finely ground in a food
  processor

2 tablespoons blanched, slivered almonds,
  finely ground in a food processor
  (omit if allergic)

8 tablespoons unsalted butter

¼ cup sugar

¼ cup brown sugar

1 large egg

1 teaspoon pure vanilla extract

¼ cup White Bean Puree (*see Make-Ahead Recipe #9*)

½ cup semi-sweet chocolate chips

Optional extra boost: **1 cup chopped walnuts or dried berries such as blueberries or raisins**

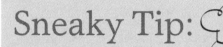

Sneaky Tip:

Double or triple this recipe and save some of the batter rolled in plastic wrap in the freezer for homemade "slice and bake" cookies anytime.

Preheat oven to 375 degrees. Remove butter from refrigerator to let soften.

In a large bowl, whisk together Flour Blend, baking soda, salt, ground oats, and ground almonds (optional). Set aside.

In the bowl of an electric mixer, beat butter and both sugars until creamy. Beat in egg, vanilla, and White Bean Puree. Add dry ingredients and mix on low speed. Stir in chocolate chips (and walnuts or dried berries, optional). Make two-bite cookies by dropping rounded *half-teaspoonfuls,* spaced 2 inches apart, onto nonstick or parchment- lined baking sheets.

Bake for 12 to 14 minutes or until golden brown. Let cool on a metal rack.

Store cookies in airtight container at room temperature.

Health-by-Chocolate Cookies

Nutrition Highlights: Whole grains, fruit, and vegetables · Rich in vitamins A, C, E, and K, potassium, manganese, folate, iron, fiber, antioxidants, and flavonoids

My mother never made spinach taste this good! Invisible in taste, texture, and appearance, both the blueberries and the spinach melt away under a blanket of delicious cocoa. And unsweetened cocoa powder not only serves the purpose of hiding the purple color of the blueberries and the spinach in the Purple Puree, but it is chock full of immunity- and mood-boosting nutrients.

As an optional extra boost, you can add whole dried blueberries at the end of the recipe. Although there is already a good dose of blueberries in the Purple Puree, it never hurts to add more of the number one healthiest fruit on Earth. Just be sure your kids won't object to seeing the whole berry in the cookie (which comes out looking more like a raisin).

MAKES ABOUT 50 TWO-BITE COOKIES

1 cup Flour Blend (see Make-Ahead Recipe #13)

½ teaspoon baking soda

½ teaspoon salt

1/4 cup unsweetened cocoa powder

8 tablespoons unsalted butter

¼ cup sugar

¼ cup brown sugar

1 large egg

1 teaspoon pure vanilla extract

6 tablespoons Purple Puree (See Make-Ahead Recipe #1)

½ cup semi-sweet chocolate chips

Optional Extra Boost: ½ cup dried blueberries or chopped walnuts

Preheat oven to 375 degrees. Remove butter from refrigerator to let soften.

In a large bowl, combine Flour Blend, baking soda, salt, and cocoa powder. Set aside.

In the bowl of an electric mixer, beat butter and both sugars until creamy. Beat in egg, vanilla, and Purple Puree. Mix in dry ingredients on low speed. Stir in chocolate chips (and walnuts or dried berries, optional). Make two-bite cookies by dropping rounded *half-teaspoonfuls*, spaced 2 inches apart, onto nonstick or parchment lined baking sheets.

Bake for 12 to 14 minutes or until golden brown. Let cool on a metal rack.

Store cookies in an airtight container at room temperature.

Brainy Brownies

Nutrition Highlights: Whole grains, fruit, and vegetables · Rich in vitamins A, C, E, and K, potassium, manganese, folate, iron, fiber, antioxidants, and flavonoids

It's hard to believe that brownies can be healthy, but this recipe "takes the cake." My baker friend Karen worked for days with me on this one and cringed every time I wanted to add another sneaky (i.e. wholesome) ingredient. Yet I knew it could be done.

*After many failed attempts, we arrived at a truly fudgy and delicious brownie that offers a solid dose of fiber from the whole wheat flour, wheat germ, and oats; antioxidants from the cocoa powder, chocolate, and blueberries; and even a good measure of iron from the spinach, which absolutely no one would guess was in there. We also managed to cut the sugar and fat to less than **half** of most brownie recipes without losing flavor.*

MAKES ABOUT 30 KID-SIZED BROWNIES

6 tablespoons unsalted butter

¾ cup semisweet chocolate chips

2 large eggs

2 teaspoons pure vanilla extract

½ cup sugar

½ cup Purple Puree (see Make-Ahead Recipe #1)

¼ cup plus 2 tablespoons Flour Blend (see Make-Ahead Recipe #13)

¼ cup rolled oats, ground in a food processor

1 tablespoon unsweetened cocoa powder

¼ teaspoon salt

Butter or non-stick cooking spray

Optional extra boost: 1 cup chopped walnuts

Preheat the oven to 350 degrees.

Butter or spray only the bottom, not the sides, of a 13-by- 9-inch or 9-inch square baking pan.

Melt the butter and chocolate chips together in a double boiler or metal bowl over simmering water (or in a microwave, checking every 15 seconds). Remove from heat and allow mixture to cool a bit. Meanwhile, in another bowl, stir together the eggs, vanilla, sugar, and Purple Puree. Combine this purple egg mixture with the cooled chocolate mixture.

In a mixing bowl, stir together Flour Blend, cocoa powder, oats, and salt. Add this to the chocolate mixture and blend thoroughly. Mix in the chopped walnuts, if using, then pour the entire mixture into the baking pan.

Bake for 30 to 35 minutes, until a toothpick comes out clean. Allow to cool completely in pan before cutting the brownies and use a plastic or butter knife. Dust with powdered sugar or sprinkles, if desired.

Keeps for a week in the refrigerator, covered tightly.

Quick Fixes for Store-Bought Chocolate Pudding

(pre-made in containers or from a box)

Nutrition Highlights: Fruit and calcium

Each nutritional booster below mixes into ¼ cup of chocolate pudding. Serve in a cup with a quick squirt of whipped cream for maximum kid appeal.

---

* ⅛ ripe avocado, pureed or mashed
   thoroughly until creamy

Rich in vitamins C and K, folate, potassium, and fiber

Make sure the avocado is very soft and ripe, but not brown. If it's not ripe enough, it will be too hard to mash with a fork and will require pureeing in the food processor. Add sprinkles to distract attention from any texture changes.

* 1 tablespoon Green Juice
   (see Make-Ahead Recipe #5)

Rich in vitamins A, K and C, manganese, folate, and iron

This looks very strange at first, but keep mixing and the green will completely disappear into the brown color of the pudding. This concoction is guaranteed to get past the pickiest eaters in town (and has won me many bets with doubting mothers)!

Quick Fix for Store-Bought Brownie Mix

If you don't have time for the scratch version, this doctored-up packaged brownie mix fits some great nutrients in. Simply replace half of the oil and all the water with nutrient-rich Purple Puree and replace some of the dry mix with wheat germ. No one I've asked, kids or adults, could tell the difference between these and the regular version.

½ cup wheat germ, unsweetened

1 box (about 21 ounces) brownie mix (preferably without hydrogenated oils)

2 large eggs

¾ cup Purple Puree (see Make-Ahead Recipe #1)

¼ cup canola oil

Preheat oven to 350 degrees. Butter or coat with cooking spray a 13-by-9-inch or 8-inch square baking pan.

Measure and discard (or save for future use) ½ cup of the dry packaged brownie mix and replace with ½ cup of wheat germ. Mix together with the eggs, oil, and Purple Puree until well blended. Follow package directions for baking time, depending on size of baking dish used.

Incredibly Improved Icing

The name says it all! These icings really are incredibly improved nutritionally. And they taste good too, so you may have a hard time convincing your mind that this usually empty food can be a concentrated source of bone-strengthening protein and calcium. In fact, with less than half of the sugar of regular icing, this healthy version is much more palatable than the sickeningly sweet stuff on most cupcakes. These icings can be made a few days ahead and stored in an airtight container in the refrigerator. When you're ready to use the icing, soften it with half a teaspoon of hot water and mix well.

Sneaky Tip:

I tested these icings with organic nonfat dry milk (Organic Valley brand, which is available at natural food stores) and with instant nonfat dry milk (Carnation brand). I found the organic version to be a bit smoother and easier to dissolve (as well as being healthier). In either case, it is critical to use boiling liquid with the recipes below.

White Icing

Nutrition Highlights: Protein and calcium · Rich in vitamin D, tryptophan, and calcium

MAKES ABOUT ¾ CUP

1 cup nonfat dry milk

½ cup powdered sugar

¼ cup **boiling** water

1 teaspoon pure vanilla extract

Mix dry milk and powdered sugar in a bowl, then add the boiling water and vanilla extract. Mix very well. If needed, add a little more water, half a teaspoon at a time, until you reach the desired consistency.

Green Icing (light in color)

Nutrition Highlights: Protein, calcium, and vegetables · Rich in vitamins A, D and K, manganese, folate, iron, tryptophan, and calcium

MAKES ABOUT ¾ CUP

¼ cup Green Juice (See Make-Ahead
   Recipe #5)

1 cup nonfat dry milk

½ cup powdered sugar

1 teaspoon lemon juice

Heat the Green Juice until just boiling (or heat in microwave on high for 30 seconds). Mix dry milk and powdered sugar in a bowl, then add the boiling Green Juice and lemon juice. Mix very well. If needed, add a little water, half a teaspoon at a time, until you reach the desired consistency.

Optional flavorings: The light green color of this icing goes well with ¼ teaspoon peppermint, almond or pistachio extract.

Lavender (Light Purple) Icing

Nutrition Highlights: protein, calcium, and fruit · Rich in vitamins C and D, tryptophan, calcium, antioxidants, and folate

MAKES ABOUT ½ CUP

¼ cup store-bought pomegranate juice or

Blueberry Juice (See Make-Ahead Recipe #6)

1 cup nonfat dry milk

½ cup powdered sugar

Heat the Blueberry Juice (or pomegranate juice) until just boiling (or heat in microwave on high for 30 seconds). Mix dry milk and powdered sugar in a bowl, then add the boiling juice. Mix very well. If needed, add a little water, half a teaspoon at a time, until you reach the desired consistency.

Chocolate Icing

Nutrition Highlights: Protein and calcium · Rich in vitamins B and D, potassium, tryptophan, antioxidants, and calcium

MAKES ABOUT ½ CUP

1 cup nonfat dry milk

½ cup powdered sugar

3 tablespoons unsweetened cocoa powder

¼ cup **boiling water**

1 teaspoon pure vanilla extract

Mix dry milk, powdered sugar, and cocoa in a bowl, then add the boiling water and vanilla extract. Mix very well. If needed, add a little more water, half a teaspoon at a time, until you reach the desired consistency.

Choc-ful Donuts / Choc-ful Cupcakes

Nutrition Highlights: whole grains, fruit, and vegetables · Rich in vitamins A, C, E and K, potassium, manganese, folate, iron, fiber, antioxidants, and flavonoids

It is my sincere belief that no child (or adult) should live cupcake-less in pursuit of a healthier lifestyle. And these cupcakes/donuts fit the bill for the look, taste, and texture of the real, decadent treat without the guilt. In fact, with entirely hidden spinach, blueberries, and wheat germ, these really do have buried treasure.

This formula makes donuts (baked, not fried) or cupcakes equally well; the only difference is the cooking vessel. When I finally invested a few dollars at the kitchen shop for a mini-bundt (a.k.a. donut) pan, a whole new world opened up to me. Suddenly all of my muffin recipes could be molded into the fun shape of forbidden donuts that can make anyone forget how healthy the ingredients are.

MAKES 12 DONUTS OR 8 CUPCAKES

4 tablespoons unsalted butter

⅓ cup (2 ounces) semisweet chocolate chips

1 large egg

2 teaspoons pure vanilla extract

¾ cup Purple Puree (See Make-Ahead Recipe #1)

½ cup sugar

1 cup Flour Blend (See Make-Ahead Recipe #13)

2 tablespoons unsweetened cocoa powder

2 teaspoons baking powder

½ teaspoon salt

Powdered sugar for dusting (for donuts)

Incredibly Improved Icing (page 244, for cupcakes)

Preheat oven to 350 degrees and spray a mini-bundt (donut) pan with oil. If you choose the cupcake option, line a muffin tin with paper liners.

Melt the butter and chocolate chips together in a double boiler or a metal bowl over simmering water (or in the microwave, checking every 15 seconds). Remove from heat and allow mixture to cool a bit. Meanwhile, in another bowl, stir together the egg, vanilla, Purple Puree, and sugar. Combine this purple egg mixture with the cooled chocolate mixture.

In a mixing bowl, stir together Flour Blend, cocoa powder, baking powder and salt. Add this to the chocolate mixture and blend thoroughly. Pour into donut molds or fill muffin cups almost to the top.

For donuts: Bake 12 to 14 minutes until the tops spring back when pressed lightly. Loosen the edges with a knife and turn the donuts out over a plate. Allow to cool, and then dust with powdered sugar or drizzle with Incredibly Improved Icing.

For cupcakes: Bake 23 to 25 minutes, until a toothpick inserted in the center comes out clean. Turn the cupcakes out of the tins to cool. Dust tops with powdered sugar or frost with Incredibly Improved Icing.

Thumbprint
Peanut Butter Cookies

Nutrition Highlights: Vegetables, whole grains, and nuts (optional) · Rich in vitamins A, B3 (niacin), C, E and K, manganese, tryptophan, iron, potassium, folate, protein, and fiber

The fingerprint of a clever sneaky chef is all over this recipe with its hidden yams and carrots pureed into the peanut butter, the ultimate flavor decoy (they also help cut the fat by less than half of traditional recipes). Crushed crunchy cereal gives the cookies more crispness than flour alone and adds a good source of nearly undetectable whole grains. You can fill the indent with a few chocolate chips or a little jam for PB&J cookies. I often double this recipe and freeze the cookies in a plastic bag for a yummy grab 'n' go snack.

MAKES 20 TO 22 COOKIES

2 cups whole grain cereal flakes (such as
  Wheaties or Total)

⅓ cup Flour Blend (see Make-Ahead
  Recipe #13)

½ teaspoon baking soda

½ teaspoon salt

1 large egg

½ cup brown sugar

3 tablespoons canola oil

¾ cup smooth peanut butter

½ cup Orange Puree (see Make-Ahead
  Recipe #2)

1 teaspoon pure vanilla extract

¼ cup semi-sweet chocolate chips or ¼ cup
  of favorite jam

Preheat oven to 400 degrees and spray a baking sheet with oil (or line with parchment paper).

Using a rolling pin, gently crush cereal (in a sealed plastic bag) into coarsely crushed flakes. Alternatively, you can quickly pulse the cereal in a food processor. In a large mixing bowl, whisk together Flour Blend, crushed cereal, baking soda, and salt. In another bowl, whisk together egg, sugar, oil, peanut butter, Orange Puree and vanilla. Add the dry ingredients to the wet and mix just until combined.

Pinch off tablespoon amounts of dough and roll about 20 balls in your hands. Place on the prepared cookie sheet about an inch apart. Gently press your thumb into the center of each ball to make an indent. Fill the indent with a few chocolate chips or a half teaspoon of jam.

Bake 16 to 18 minutes, or until golden brown.

Say Yes to Sorbet

Nutrition highlights: Fruit and fiber · Rich in vitamins C and K, fiber, antioxidants, and ellagic acid

*My kids (and even I) want dessert nearly every night after dinner. I got tired of saying no all the time and enduring the fights and negotiations. Instead, I decided to get creative and use this daily request as an opportunity to not only win the "best mom" award, but also to slip in another serving of immune-boosting fruit for the day. With your mini food processor on hand, this homemade sorbet takes less than two minutes prep time. Serve in a parfait or ice cream glass and garnish with a few colored sprinkles. This recipe can be quickly converted to a thinner **virgin fruit daiquiri** by adding an extra ½ cup of juice and then mixing in the blender. Serve with a straw and cocktail umbrella, if you're feeling especially festive.*

MAKES 2 SERVINGS

1½ cups frozen strawberries, blueberries, or cherries (without syrup or added sweeteners)

½ cup store-bought pomegranate juice, or Blueberry, Cherry, or Strawberry Juice (See Make-Ahead Recipes #6, 7, or 8)

2 teaspoons sugar or honey

Put all ingredients in food processor and puree on high—hold on tight, the first few seconds are a bit rough until the mixture smoothes out.

DRINKS

Milkshakes 4 Ways

Why deprive children of delicious milkshakes, if you can use them as a delivery system for some healthy nutrients? Try to get away with using a good, low-fat frozen yogurt as the base for these shakes. If that won't work, choose a light ice cream with a bit less fat. Although these are a little too sweet for breakfast (smoothies are better), all of the variations provide an excellent source of calcium, and with the added fruits and vegetables, you've got an absolutely delicious, deceptively healthy snack or dessert.

Earth Day Milk Shake

Nutrition Highlights: Calcium and vegetables · Rich in vitamins A, C, and K, manganese, folate, iron, calcium, and protein

Yes, it's bright green, but so are mint chocolate chip and pistachio ice creams—and that never stood in anyone's way. Tell the kids you're celebrating Earth Day or St. Patrick's Day or just having fun. They will gobble it up and you'll be amazed. The key is to start with a really good tasting vanilla frozen yogurt or light ice cream; the vanilla extract will help its flavor shine through. Each tablespoon of Green Juice is the equivalent of eating about ¼ cup of spinach or collard greens, so you can feel great

about serving this delicious treat. Start with the lesser amount of juice called for, and work up to more over time.

MAKES 2 SERVINGS

2 cups vanilla low-fat ice cream or
   frozen yogurt
4 to 6 tablespoons Green Juice
   (See Make-Ahead Recipe #5)
¼ cup milk
½ teaspoon pure vanilla extract

Blend all ingredients together in a blender until smooth. Serve in tall glasses with a quick squirt of whipped cream and a straw.

Chocolate Shake

Nutrition Highlights: Calcium and vegetables • Rich in vitamins A, C, and K, manganese, folate, iron, calcium, and protein

MAKES 2 SERVINGS

2 cups chocolate low-fat ice cream or
   frozen yogurt
4 to 6 tablespoons Green Juice
   (See Make-Ahead Recipe #5)
¼ cup milk
½ teaspoon pure vanilla extract

Blend all ingredients together in a blender until smooth. Serve in tall glasses with a quick squirt of whipped cream and a straw.

Creamy Chocolate Shake

Nutrition Highlights: Calcium and fruit • Rich in vitamins C and K, folate, potassium, fiber, and calcium.
This one continues to amaze me. Avocado—technically a fruit but with the nutrients of a vegetable—lends a creaminess to this shake, yet it leaves almost no detectable taste beneath the chocolate.

MAKES 2 SERVINGS

2 cups chocolate low-fat ice cream or
   frozen yogurt
¼ ripe avocado

¼ cup milk
½ teaspoon pure vanilla extract

Blend all ingredients together in a blender until smooth. Serve in tall glasses with a quick squirt of whipped cream and a straw.

Blue Ribbon Shake

Nutrition Highlights: Calcium and fruit • Rich in vitamins A and C, potassium, folate, flavonoids, calcium, and antioxidants

They have to like the taste of blueberry for this one, although since you'll be using only the juice from the berries, there will be no objectionable leafiness or pulp.

MAKES 2 SERVINGS

2 cups vanilla low-fat ice cream or
   frozen yogurt
6 tablespoons Blueberry Juice
   (See Make-Ahead Recipe #6)
¼ cup milk
½ teaspoon pure vanilla extract

Blend all ingredients together in a blender until smooth. Serve in tall glasses with a quick squirt of whipped cream and a straw.

Flavored Milk 3 Ways

The popularity of flavored milk has soared recently, since fast-food chains replaced plain milk in paper cartons with plastic bottles of sweet flavored milks. As of 2006, fast-food chains have sold an average of more than 5 million units per week, compared to the 690,000 units per week that were sold when the milk was offered in paper cartons.

This is both a blessing and a curse. Flavored milk does give children the calcium they need, in a form they'll actually drink, and may crowd out less healthy beverages such as soda and fruit drinks. One study reported by the American Dietetic Association certainly found that children who consume flavored milk have higher calcium intakes than those who don't. However, this beverage comes with a price, since in general, flavored milks contain loads of artificial flavors and colors, along with sweeteners such as high fructose corn syrup.

The following recipes offer all of the benefits with none of the disadvantages. Kids will drink more milk, but these are sweetened with nutrient-dense real fruit juices and contain no artificial ingredients.

Strawberry Milk

Nutrition Highlights: *fruit and calcium* · Rich in vitamins C, D, and K, manganese, iodine, tryptophan, calcium, and fiber

MAKES 2 SERVINGS

2 cups milk

6 to 8 tablespoons Strawberry Juice
   (see Make-Ahead Recipe #8)

Stir all ingredients together until well combined. Serve in favorite cups with straws.

Chocolate Milk

Nutrition Highlights: Fruit and calcium · Rich in vitamins A, C, and D, potassium, iodine, tryptophan, calcium, and antioxidants

Cherry and chocolate is the best combination I've found and the juice is barely noticeable. If anything, the cherry adds depth to the chocolate and enhances its flavor.

MAKES 2 SERVINGS

2 cups milk

6 to 8 tablespoons Cherry Juice
   (see Make-Ahead Recipe #7)

1 tablespoon chocolate syrup

Stir all ingredients together until well combined. Serve in favorite cups with straws.

Blueberry Milk

Nutrition Highlights: Fruit and calcium · Rich in vitamins C, D and E, iodine, tryptophan, manganese, antioxidants, calcium, and fiber

MAKES 2 SERVINGS

2 cups milk

6 to 8 tablespoons Blueberry Juice
   (see Make-Ahead Recipe #6)

Stir all ingredients together until well combined. Serve in favorite cups with straws.

Quick Fixes for Store-Bought Lemonade

Try to choose lemonade that doesn't have artificial colors, flavors, or high fructose corn syrup (or this works with homemade lemonade). Mix one of the following with 1 cup of lemonade:

---

* ¼ to ½ cup Blueberry Juice

   (See Make-Ahead Recipe #6)

Rich in vitamins C and E, manganese, and antioxidants

* ¼ to ½ cup Cherry Juice

   (see Make-Ahead Recipe #7)

Rich in vitamins A, C, potassium, and antioxidants

* ¼ to ½ cup Strawberry Juice

   (see Make-Ahead Recipe #8)

Rich in vitamins C, K, manganese, antioxidants, and fiber.

* ¼ to ½ cup store-bought pomegranate juice

Rich in A, C, and E, iron, and antioxidants

* ¼ to ½ cup unsweetened (decaf) black tea

Rich in vitamin C and flavonoids

* ¼ to ½ cup unsweetened (decaf) green tea

Rich in vitamin C and flavonoids

Cheery Hot Cocoa

Nutrition Highlights: Fruit and calcium · Rich in vitamins A, C and D, tryptophan, potassium, calcium, and antioxidants

*Cherry, informally known as the "healing fruit," not only significantly boosts the nutritional benefits of this delicious kid-favorite treat, but it also quietly enhances the rich taste of the cocoa. This cherry hot cocoa really is **cheery**, since cocoa has been found to elevate moods and warm the spirit, especially after sledding on snowy winter days. I keep frozen cherries all year long so we don't have to wait for the fresh ones during those few summer months.*

MAKES 2 SERVINGS

2 cups milk

2 tablespoons sugar

Pinch salt

1 tablespoon unsweetened
cocoa powder

½ teaspoon pure vanilla
extract

½ cup Cherry Juice (See
Make-Ahead Recipe #7)

Optional toppings: **mini
marshmallows, whipped
cream**

Combine milk, sugar, salt, and cocoa powder in a pot and warm over low heat. Stir occasionally until well combined and turn off heat when you reach desired temperature (before boiling). Stir in vanilla and Cherry Juice, then serve warm with optional toppings.

Alternatively, mix milk, sugar, salt, and cocoa powder in a microwave safe bowl and heat in the microwave on high for 30 seconds at a time until desired temperature. Mix in vanilla and Cherry Juice, then serve warm in mugs with optional toppings.

Quick Fixes for Sparkling Water

Nutrition Highlights: fruit and antioxidants

The average American drinks an estimated fifty-six gallons of soft drinks each year. In the past ten years, soft drink consumption among children has almost doubled in the United States. This has, undoubtedly, led to the increase in obesity among kids. One can of soda has about ten teaspoons of sugar, 150 calories, and loads artificial food colors, caffeine, and sulfites. Whatever we can do to keep kids away from the stuff is good.

Even the new natural sodas on the market provide too many calories in the form of sweeteners and too much sugar for the waistline and teeth. Below are fast recipes for sparkling water mixed with our homemade nutrient-rich fruit juices, and they make an excellent alternative to sugary sodas. I mix the juice and seltzer in small water bottles for the kids to take to school, and they seem to enjoy it even more than traditional juice boxes.

Mix equal parts sparkling water and any of the below juices:

---

*Blueberry Juice (See Make-Ahead Recipe #6)

Rich in vitamins C and E, manganese, and antioxidants

*Cherry Juice (See Make-Ahead Recipe #7)

Rich in vitamins A and C, potassium, and antioxidants

*Strawberry Juice (see Make-Ahead Recipe #8)

Rich in vitamins C and K, manganese, antioxidants, and fiber

* Store-bought pomegranate juice

Rich in A, C and E, iron, and antioxidants

Congratulations to all you new "sneaky chefs." You have embarked on an adventurous and admirable campaign to improve your family's health. This may be the end of the book, but it is only the beginning of your new way of life. Feel free to pass your knowledge on to others. In your own way, you are participating in the growing movement to transform the way America feeds its children.

As I've said, it's easy to be a sneaky chef—the only hard part is keeping a straight face. Have fun!

Acknowledgments

I would like to thank so many special people in my life who have made important contributions to this book. First is the tireless team of taste testers, whose excitement and enthusiasm was always up to the Sneaky Chef Challenge: Ariana, Veronica, Sofie, Jesse, Callie, Leo, Josh, Sammy, Daphne, Constantine, Rebecca, Jenna, Amy and Rich, Logan, Alex, Jessica, Melanie, Peri, Matthew, Julia, Jeff, Sharon, Benjamin and Rachel, Daniel, Eric, Elly, Brigitte, and Bryan.

Right beside me throughout this process is the group of people that have given me constant inspiration and guidance: My mother, who taught me how to eat for health and for logging countless hours in the test kitchen; my Dad, who gave me the skills and fortitude to execute my dreams; my sister, Karen, who always believes in me; my brother, Larry Chase, my spiritual twin and constant guide on our path; my stepmother, Ulla, a great cook and my teacher in the kitchen; my dear friends, Karen Ganz, who generously gave me her time and secrets to great tasting food, and Robert Rosenthal, the *KitchenMC*, who taught me how to have fun in the kitchen; my stepdaughter, Rachel Lapine, who is a gifted graphic designer and friend; and my wonderful test kitchen manager, Jean Buckhan, who always keeps me calm and organized.

I am very grateful to chef Daniel Boulud, who sets the standard of excellence for chefs worldwide and whose support of me made all the difference; to my incomparable agents, Joelle Delbourgo and Molly Lyons, whose expertise and support made sure this groundbreaking book would reach the marketplace; and to my brilliant editor, Jennifer Kasius, and the exceptional team at Running Press, Jon Anderson, Craig Herman, and Bill Jones, who understood the vision of this book from the start and stayed true to its message.

A special thanks to author Susan Page, whose book, *The Shortest Distance Between You and a Published Book,* generously guided me through the publishing process; terrific legal advisor, Sheila Levine; excellent nutritionist, Geri Brewster; and my invaluable book consultant, Amanita Rosenbush, whose expertise in editing book proposals and organizing the material for the manuscript ensured that this book would get published.

Thanks to Gary Goldberg, Executive Director of the *New School Culinary Arts,* for seeing the value of this method and making me a part of his faculty; to exceptional editors Andrea Messina and Janet Chan of *Parenting Magazine,* who supported this book early on; to Alison Meiseles and her team, for their time and expertise to create our television pilot; to Floor Van Herreweghe for designing a fantastic website; to stellar food photographer, Jerry Errico, and five-star food stylist and chef, Brian Preston-Campbell; and a special thanks to Kristopher Weber who created the winning logo. My special thanks to Kim Perry at Alliance for a Healthier Generation, a partnership between the American Heart Association and the William J. Clinton Foundation, for allowing me to contribute toward their important work helping schools serve healthier lunches.

I am so grateful for the love and support of dear friends who stood by me as this idea came alive: Carolyn Kremins, Robert Rosenthal, Laura Klein, Frank Rimler, Risa and Steve Goldberg, Denise Gotsdiner, Andy Clibanoff, Stacey Kornfeld, Abby and Bruce Mendelsohn, Karen Ganz, Robert Sutner, Jackie Geller, Petra Kaufman, Tassos Koumbourlis, and Judy Fox.

And last on the list which means first in my heart, my most heartfelt gratitude goes to my always supportive husband and best friend, Rick Lapine, and our shining stars, Emily and Samantha.

I am sincerely grateful to all of you.

Dear Readers,

Thank you for sharing your time with us, and for making *The Sneaky Chef* a part of your family's life. To share your ideas and comments with other parents and me, and for new recipes, tips, special promotions, and appearance dates, please come visit us at:

www.TheSneakyChef.com

I also invite you to share your experience with this method and your own sneaky ideas by emailing me at **Missy@TheSneakyChef.com.** And you may also send me your funny and interesting home video or CD of any sneaky chef moments—good or bad—and share how your family is doing to:

The Sneaky Chef
PO Box 117
Ardsley on Hudson, NY 10503

As often as possible, I will upload these videos on my website and my viewers can vote on which family will receive free personal coaching from me.

Index

RECIPES LISTED
BY MAKE-AHEAD
INGREDIENT